EMPORIUM of the NORTH

Peace R.

Rivière des Roches

Revillon Coupé

Chenal des Quatre Fourches

BARIL LAKE

Mission Creek

Head Bog

Ft. Chipewyan (1797)

Fraser B.

Ft. Chipew
(18

X X Fort
Nottingham House

Mission Pt.
LOBSTICK I.
MOUSE I.
POTATO I.

Ft. Weddeburn

LAKE
CLAIRE

MAMAWI LAKE

Hilda
Lake

Channel

Fletcher

Embarras R.

Athabasca

Limon Lake

RICHARDS
LAKE

Blanche
Lake

Lillian Wonders

Pond's Fort

EMPORIUM
of the NORTH

Fort Chipewyan and the Fur Trade to 1835

by James Parker

**Alberta Culture and Multiculturalism/
Canadian Plains Research Center
1987**

To the people of Fort Chipewyan

Canadian Cataloguing in Publication Data

Parker, James McPherson, 1934-
    Emporium of the north : Fort Chipewyan and the fur
trade to 1835

    Bibliography: p.
    Includes index.
    ISBN 0-88977-0441

    1. Fort Chipewyan (Alta.)—History. 2. Fur trade—
Canada, Western—History. 3. Fur trade—Canada,
Northern—History. 4. Northwest, Canadian—History—
To 1870.* I. University of Regina. Canadian Plains
Research Center. II. Alberta. Alberta Culture and Multiculturalism
III. Title.
FC3213.P37 1987   971.23′201   C87-098047-5
F1060.8.P37 1987

CONTENTS

LIST OF ILLUSTRATIONS

LIST OF TABLES

FOREWORD

It is at least a generation since Jim Parker began his work at Fort Chipewyan and nearly nineteen years since he presented his thesis for the degree of Master of Arts. There can be no doubt that it has stood the test of time. It has been read, quoted and possibly even plagiarized by a generation of students of the fur trade and the northwest. It remains an authoritative source for the history of one of the most famous of the fur trade posts of the Canadian northwest.

The study is also of particular interest in the development of graduate study in history at the University of Alberta. While Mr. Parker was a student, the staff of the Department grew rapidly, from eleven in 1959 to twenty-one in 1967-68. The demand for courses in Canadian history had grown even more rapidly and so had the demand for advanced work in Canadian history generally and in western Canadian history particularly. In light of this, we reorganized our course offerings and effectively restricted the course in the history of the Canadian west to students with some prior experience of university courses in history generally. This, we thought, perhaps naïvely, would free staff time for graduate supervision.

Dr. W.J. Eccles, who had played an active part in this reshaping and redirecting of our resources, suggested that what the fur trade period of western history needed was studies of individual fur trade posts with an emphasis upon the life of their people. This would move the history of the fur trade into the stream of Canadian social history and away from the view that it was simply an aspect of British Empire business history. He suggested that Mr. Parker might devote himself to Fort Chipewyan, an important post whose records were comparatively available to a student working from an Edmonton base. Parker took up the challenge and, following the precepts of Arthur S. Morton, not only scrutinized the primary documents and available secondary material, but spent a year teaching in Fort Chipewyan and thoroughly familiarizing himself with the terrain. His modest reference in his preface to his Chipewyan experience should not be allowed to conceal the devotion with which he and Mrs. Parker involved themselves in the life of that historic community.

Parker's account of Fort Chipewyan was a step in the direction of a reorientation and enrichment of the history of the Canadian west before 1870, a process that assists in a clearer understanding of the development of Canada in the post-Confederation period. With the work of scholars like John E. Foster, Sylvia Van Kirk, Frits Pannekoek, and John Nicks, to mention only four who had a close connection with the University of Alberta, it helped to bring the collectivity of scholarship to a new insight into the fur trade and a new appreciation of the relationships between the variety of elements in the western community that the trade brought into contact. This new insight was the more penetrating because it interacted with the works of the other disciplines, among them anthropology, archaeology, geography and sociology, that were increasingly active in the Canadian west.

L.G. Thomas
January, 1986

PREFACE

Fort Chipewyan, the first European settlement in Alberta, was ideally situated for the fur trade, located as it is at the hub of a drainage system. The fort was reached from the south by the Athabasca River, and the streams running to the north and to the west became highways for expansion of the trade. Lake Athabasca stretches to the east. As a base for extending the trade, Fort Chipewyan ranked second, surpassed only by Fort William on Lake Superior. Not only the fur trade benefitted from the establishment of Fort Chipewyan, however, because as the "Grand Magazine of the North" it became the base of operations for land explorers. Alexander Mackenzie, John Franklin, George Back, and John Richardson were a few of the men who gained fame after passing through its gates.

This study examines the establishment of the fur trade at Lake Athabasca, with Fort Chipewyan as its focus. It covers the period from the entry of Peter Pond in 1778, to 1835. By then, the fur trade had recovered from the damaging effects of the competition between the North West Company and the Hudson's Bay Company that preceded their amalgamation in 1821. The study portrays the life of a fort as it was related to the fur trade of a district. Fort Chipewyan, headquarters of both the North West Company's and Hudson's Bay Company's Athabasca enterprises, offers an opportunity to examine the fur trade under the differing conditions prior to and after 1821. Although documents are lacking for the North West period, there are sufficient records to indicate the conditions of the trade.

Two volumes edited by L.F.R. Masson are particularly helpful. They contain the reminiscences of Roderick Mackenzie, James Mackenzie's 1799-1800 journal at Fort Chipewyan, and Ferdinand Wentzell's letters to Roderick Mackenzie, all of which provide considerable information on the early history of the Athabasca district. Philip Turnor's journal of his Lake Athabasca expedition in 1790-92, published by the Champlain Society, has some excellent information on the North West Company's organization and trading methods. Peter Fidler's Nottingham House Journals (1802-06) provide a description of the conflict between the Canadian companies. There are no accounts of the 1806-14 years at Fort Chipewyan. Nevertheless, the Minutes of the North West Company in the Champlain Society volume edited by W.S. Wallace indicate the difficulties experienced in the Athabasca trade. The letters of Ferdinand Wentzell also give an idea of conditions in the Athabasca before and during the 1815-21 struggle.

The Selkirk Papers in the Public Archives of Canada contain journals and papers captured at Fort William in 1816. The John McLeod and C.N. Bell collection contain some Fort Chipewyan letters as do the North West Company Papers in the Hudson's Bay Company Archives, Provincial Archives of Manitoba. The Hudson's Bay Company Archives also provide detailed records of the fort after 1821.

The study was extended to 1835 partly because several of the explorers' narratives could be used. Furthermore, by 1835 the fur trade had recovered from the damaging effects of the pre-1821 competition.

I am indebted to Frits Pannekoek, director, Historic Sites Service, Alberta Culture and Multiculturalism, who encouraged publication; to Patricia Myers, for her close editorial attention; and to Carl Betke and Richard Goulet at Historic Sites Service and Gillian Wadsworth Minifie and Brian Mlazgar, at Canadian Plains Research Center, for final preparation of the manuscript.

The photographs of trade goods and fur trade artifacts were taken by Karie Hardie of the Archaeological Survey of Alberta with the assistance of Patricia Myers, Historic Sites Service. Robert Kidd and Maurice Doll of the Provincial Museum of Alberta generously provided assistance with the selection of artifacts and trade goods. The maps were drawn by Lillian Wonders of the Department of Geography,

University of Alberta.

I wish to express my thanks to the Governor and Committee of the Hudson's Bay Company for their kind permission to use the microfilm records at the Public Archives in Ottawa, and to consult the North West Papers. I am indebted to the Provincial Archives of Alberta for access to its Fort Chipewyan journals. I wish further to thank the administrators of the John S. Ewart Memorial Fund for a grant which made my research in Ottawa possible.

My thanks go to the people of Fort Chipewyan, especially Messrs. Roderick Fraser, Paul Kelpin, Frank Ladouceur, Horace Wylie, and Lawrence Yanik, and Noel Mackay and Victor Mercredi, now deceased, whose friendships and assistance during my year at Fort Chipewyan led to a better understanding of my subject. A journey by canoe from Fort McMurray to Fort Chipewyan proved of great benefit in the writing of this study.

I also extend my thanks to W.J. Eccles, now Professor Emeritus of the University of Toronto, who recommended this topic to me.

Finally, I express my deepest appreciation to Professor Lewis G. Thomas of the University of Alberta for his valuable counsel and encouragement in the development of this study.

James Parker, 1987

1. INTRODUCTION

During the last two decades of the eighteenth century, the fur trade reached the Athabasca country. The "Athabasca" was first used to describe the Mackenzie River basin, being the land drained by waters flowing into the Arctic Ocean. The North West Company in 1802 set its boundaries 55° north latitude to 66° north latitude and 110° west longitude to 120° west longitude.[1] The northeastern corner crossed the Burnside River near the mouth of the Cracroft River, District of Mackenzie; the southeastern corner fixed upon Primrose Lake, Saskatchewan. The northwestern corner was Great Bear Lake, District of Mackenzie, and the southwestern corner was a few miles west of Beaverlodge, Alberta. The district included the Peace River, Athabasca River, Slave River, and Mackenzie River systems.[2]

The permanent establishment of a post here marked a deep penetration into the far northwest. Founded in 1788, Fort Chipewyan, on Lake Athabasca, still functions as a fur trade post although its importance has declined from the days when Alexander Mackenzie termed it the "Emporium of the North." In 1791, while surveying Lake Athabasca for the Hudson's Bay Company, Philip Turnor described the fort as "the compleatest Inland House I have seen in the country . . . the Grand Magazine of the Athapiscow Country."[3] With a two years' supply of goods in store, the fort held a commanding position as entrepot in the expanding fur trade of the Athabasca.[4]

Today, Fort Chipewyan has fallen victim to the passage of time. The last of the old buildings dating from the 1870s, the former residence of the chief factor, was torn down in August, 1964. One can only wander along fading footpaths between the still visible outlines of buildings that were removed in 1939. The main path leads from the site of the old buildings across the outline of the east stockade up to the high rocky point, known as "the rock," where the lookout

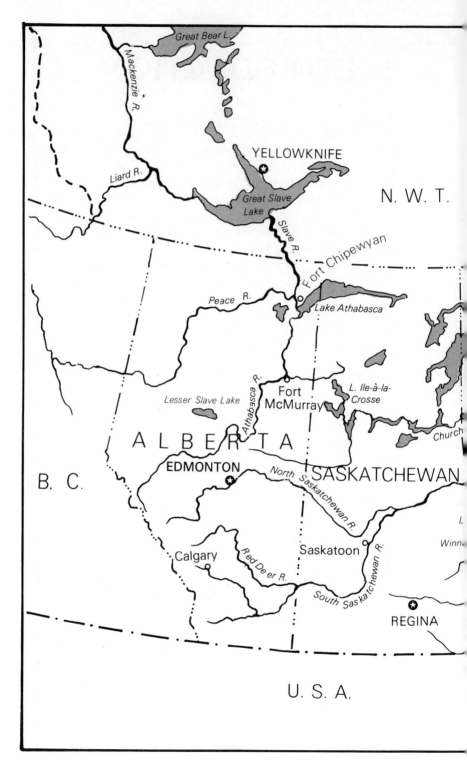

Great Bear L.

Mackenzie R.

YELLOWKNIFE

Liard R.

N. W. T.

Great Slave
Lake

Slave R.

Fort Chipewyan

Peace R.

Lake Athabasca

Athabasca R.

Lesser Slave Lake

Fort
McMurray

L. Ile-à-la-
Crosse

A L B E R T A

Church

EDMONTON

North Saskatchewan R.

SASKATCHEWAN

B. C.

Calgary

Red Deer R.

Saskatoon

South Saskatchewan R.

L.

Winn.

REGINA

U. S. A.

PRAIRIE PROVINCES
(and surrounding area)

100   0   100   200   300

MILES

HUDSON BAY

NITOBA

Southern
ndian Lake

Nelson R.

Severn R.

James
Bay

ONTARIO

Albany R.

Lake
Winnipeg

ake
toba

Lake Nipigon

WINNIPEG

Thunder Bay

Sault
Ste Marie

Red R.

tower and the powder magazine once stood.[5] Here stands the base of the fort sundial which faithfully marked time until the 1940s. Southeast across the lake where willows fringe the shore, can be seen the outline of Goose Island. The island, lying in shallow, reed-choked water near the mouth of the silt-laden Athabasca River, can only hint at its former importance as a fort fishery. Beyond Goose Island, Old Fort Point, the first site of Fort Chipewyan, can be distinguished on clear days. A mirage frequently forms and magnifies the proportions of both the island and the point.

Two miles to the southwest of "the rock" are the entrances to the Rocher River and the Quatre Fourches. Between them lies English Island where Peter Fidler failed in his attempt to establish a permanent post for the Hudson's Bay Company. Looking directly west, Dog Head, a massive hill of granite, juts into the lake. About a mile away, nothing remains of the XY Company's post on Little Island, a piece of rock separated by only a few feet of water from Mission Point, known locally as "Colin Fraser's Point." One mile south of "the rock," across the channel of water leading out of the lake, sits Potato (formerly Coal) Island, whose somber, spruce-covered hills scarcely give a hint that they once harboured Fort Wedderburn, witness to the final struggle between the Hudson's Bay Company and the North West Company.

The land around Fort Chipewyan today has changed little since the coming of the white man. Its ruggedness and solitude are strong reminders of the days when Fort Chipewyan was the emporium of the district that E.E. Rich termed "the Eldorado of the north-west."[6]

The fur trade expanded towards the far northwest from its bases on Hudson Bay and the St. Lawrence-Great Lakes system. When the Montrealers, or pedlars, reached the Saskatchewan and Churchill rivers in the 1760s, they precipitated a clash between two competing economies. There they could intercept the Indians carrying furs intended for trade with the Hudson's Bay Company's posts on the

Bay. The intervention of the Montreal traders upset a well-developed system of inland trade that extended through Chipewyan and Cree middlemen to the Athabasca, Dogrib, and Copper Indians of the far northwest.[7] This method of trade dated back to 1691 when Henry Kelsey had first journeyed inland to bring the Indians and their furs down to Hudson Bay. The northern Indians were introduced into this trade system in the early eighteenth century when James Knight sent William Stewart and Richard Norton inland from Churchill.[8] Although the Hudson's Bay Company did not establish permanent inland posts until after the Montrealers began to intercept the Indian brigades, it is worth noting that the northern Indian in all likelihood received his first view of European civilization through the Bay. It is also worth noting at this point that, from its beginning, the Hudson's Bay Company determined the value of its furs and trade goods in terms of prime winter beaver pelts, called "made beaver."

During the 1770s it became increasingly clear to the pedlars that the country north of the Saskatchewan harboured a vast number of furs. In 1771 and 1772 Thomas Corry, the first of the pedlars, intercepted Indian brigades on the Saskatchewan.[9] His retirement after two successful seasons of trade was probably an incentive to the traders who followed his trail in 1773. The Frobisher brothers, with the aid of Louis Primeau, were instrumental in making the first approach to the Athabasca. Primeau undoubtedly supplied information regarding the Churchill River, since he apparently wintered along this system for the Hudson's Bay Company in 1775-76.[10] Thomas Frobisher wintered in Ile-à-la-Crosse Lake in 1775-76.[11] The success of the Frobishers, especially in intercepting the trade to the Bay, stood as a testimonial to the existence of a rich source of furs in the upper Churchill country and the unexplored regions beyond Ile-à-la-Crosse.[12] The success of the Quebec traders may be attributed to their practice of offering goods at lower prices and in greater quantity than the organization of Indian middlemen who extorted high prices from the Indians of the far northwest.[13]

When the Frobisher brothers retired from the interior with their fortunes, the redoubtable Peter Pond, who had been on the Saskatchewan since 1775, formed a "concern" with six other pedlars at Sturgeon Fort in 1778.

> Seven fur-traders . . . he considered far too many to be living at one trading establishment; and he believed . . . that he could realize a larger profit if he and the men employed by him alone could reach the centre of the Chipewyan country at or near Lake Athabasca.[14]

With the five canoes provided by the partnership, Pond made his approach through the Churchill River system, over the Portage La Loche (Methy Portage) separating the Hudson Bay and Arctic drainage basins, and down the Clearwater River to the Athabasca River, where, on a point some forty miles south of Lake Athabasca, he spent the winter of 1778-79 trading furs.

Before Pond reached the Athabasca, Moses Norton, Governor of Churchill Fort, gave evidence of the Hudson's Bay Company's concerns with the threat to the Athabasca trade posed by the pedlars by sending Joseph Hansom inland along the Churchill River to rally the Indians to the Bay posts. When Hansom returned with the Indian brigades in 1774, he was intercepted at Frog Portage (Portage de Traite) by Joseph Frobisher.[15] Although Samuel Hearne reported in 1777 that his policy of dispatching Indians to trade in the Athabasca country had increased the yield at Churchill to eleven thousand made beaver from an annual average of six thousand,[16] the results of the attempts to regain the Athabasca trade at Cumberland House, the first inland post of the Hudson's Bay Company on the Saskatchewan, were discouraging.[17] Handicapped by the lack of men, canoes, and trade goods, the Company was unable to take the initiative in the interior.[18] The Montrealers held a dominant position in the trade of the 1780s.

A series of disasters struck the Hudson's Bay Company in the early 1780s. Smallpox, apparently carried from the

Mississippi country by the Snake Indians, ravaged the entire Indian population in 1781. The fur trade in the northwest was severely affected. The War of American Independence reached into Hudson Bay with the devastating sea attacks of the French navy under Jean-Françoise de Galaup, comte de Lapérouse on York and Churchill forts, ruining the trade at Churchill. Mattonabbee, leader of the northern Indians, committed suicide in despair over the capture of his English friends. These disasters and Pond's first expedition stalled plans for an immediate expansion into the Athabasca.

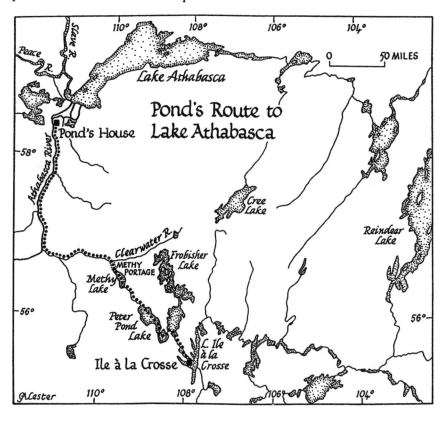

Peter Pond was the first white man to travel to the Athabasca district to trade for furs with the Indians. This map shows his route, which included crossing the difficult Methy Portage. (Provincial Archives of Alberta)

Peter Pond's expeditions to the Athabasca in 1780, 1781 and 1783, led him to formulate the idea of exploring north from the Athabasca in hopes of reaching the Pacific Ocean.[19] His idea was a result of the recent discovery of an inlet (Cook's Inlet) by James Cook on the northwest coast of America. Cook believed that his inlet was the mouth of a large river from the interior. In 1785 Pond petitioned Lieutenant-Governor Hamilton of Lower Canada for government support of an expedition to seek the way to the Pacific Ocean; his petition also included a request for a monopoly on his route to the Athabasca and the fur trade of that region.[20] Although the government was impressed by Pond's ideas, no official privileges were given to the fur trader-explorer, nor did the recently formed North West Company gain any official support for its project.[21]

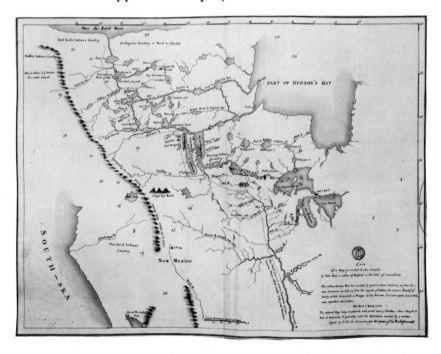

Peter Pond's 1785 map of what is now western Canada. This map encouraged other explorers to venture into the northwest and beyond. (Public Archives of Canada, National Map Collection, PH/700/1785)

TABLE 1

Athabasca Outfits and Returns 1778 - Peter Pond

Outfit

No. of Canoes	Men	Estimated Pieces* of Trade Goods
5	25	100

Returns

No. of Packs	Weight of Pack	Made Beaver	Estimated Value†
140	90 lbs.	8,400	£ 8,400

Eleven canoes would carry about 220 packs of furs‡ with an approximate value of £13,200.

Source: Cumberland House Journals Second Series, 1779-1782, Hudson's Bay Record Society, vol. 15, pp. 6 and 6n, 2 July 1779; E.E. Rich, *History of the Hudson's Bay Company*, vol. 2, 76.

* A "piece" refers to a 90 lb. bale of trade goods.

† The estimated value of these tables is based upon the value of a fur pack varying between £30 and £90 sterling. An average of £60 per pack has been set. The estimated value does not mean gross or net profit (see Appendix).

In 1789 Alexander Mackenzie told the North West agents:

You will observe by the amount of Goods remaining here that there are more than sufficiency [sic] for another year—Therefore it will be needless to send any more canoes in, than will be required to carry out the Returns—Eight with three of the five Canoes that remains [sic] in hand will carry more than the Country will produce (L.R. Masson, *Bourgeois*, vol. 1, Reminiscences of R. Mackenzie, p. 30, A. Mackenzie to Agents of the North West Company, dated Athabaska, 22 May 1789).

‡ The estimate is based upon an average of 20 packs per canoe. *Cf.*, W.S. Wallace, *Documents*, 252.

Since Pond's initial Athabasca enterprise yielded him at least eight thousand made beaver (see Table 1), other pedlars were quick to enter the country. The approach to the Athabasca in the 1780s was marked by strife and bloodshed. In 1782, Jean Etienne Waden was killed at Lac La Ronge in a trading dispute with Peter Pond. Acquitted of this murder in Montreal, Pond became implicated in the violent death of John Ross in the Athabasca country in 1787.[22] These tragedies seemed to have a sobering effect on the Montrealers. The principal trading concerns made an agreement in the same year to form a greater North West Company.[23]

That the Montrealers had not yet resolved the problem of an approach to the Athabasca country is evident from Alexander Mackenzie's observation of 1788:

> It is difficult to say what can be done in time to come in this country, but, as far as can be judged from present appearances, there will be no possibility of establishing a fort there to advantage, nor could the produce come out the same year. I am certain, if the Chipeweans could be drawn away from there, the other nations would draw near, and if a *rendez-vous* could be established, an advantageous trade would be carried on. . . .[24]

Although Mackenzie was referring to the discouraging prospects for trade on Great Slave Lake, the necessity for a *rendez-vous* was clear to him by the summer of 1788. The possibility of the existence of a river which would provide a route to the Pacific Ocean was foremost in Mackenzie's thoughts. The exploration he envisioned would only be practical if there could be a base of operations in the Athabasca. Any exploratory venture would then be shortened by having an outfit of provisions and supplies in the far northwest. The base would naturally also serve as his proposed *rendez-vous* for the Athabasca Indians. His cousin, Roderick Mackenzie, describes the outcome:

> He then informed me, in confidence, that he had determined on undertaking a voyage of discovery the ensuing spring by the water communications reported to lead from Slave Lake

to the Northern Ocean, adding that if I could not return and take charge of his department in his absence, he must abandon his intention. . . . I, without hesitation, accompanied him into Athabasca. . . .[25]

In the fall of that year, Roderick Mackenzie established Fort Chipewyan on Lake Athabasca.[26]

The formidable threat posed by a united opposition based in Montreal had not gone unheeded by the London Adventurers. The Hudson's Bay Company had sufficiently recouped its losses by 1789 to plan at least two expeditions to the Athabasca. An exploring party under Charles Duncan was to search for an approach by sea through Chesterfield Inlet and Wager Bay. This project ended in failure when an unfit vessel faced ice conditions and a closed coastline.[27] A second expedition was directed to follow the Canadians' approach from Cumberland House on the Saskatchewan. Philip Turnor, the Company's first full time surveyor, assumed leadership of this party. Accompanied by Malchom Ross and Peter Fidler, he began to survey the route inland from Cumberland more or less following a North West brigade under Patrick Small to Ile-à-la-Crosse, where both parties wintered in 1790-91. Turnor was handicapped by a lack of provision posts *en route*; his party was obliged to live off the land. Turnor meant to travel over Methy Portage but, warned by the North West brigade of the lack of provisions at the Portage, he decided, on the advice of his Chipewyan guides, to travel from the Methy River up Garson River to Garson Lake. Then, his party travelled down the rapid-strewn Christina River to the Clearwater, near its junction with the Athabasca.[28] Turnor's survey of Lake Athabasca and the Slave River, his stay near the Northwesters at Fort Chipewyan, and Peter Fidler's winter travels with the Chipewyans on Great Slave Lake contributed immensely to the London Committee's knowledge of the Athabasca country.

Philip Turnor left the Athabasca convinced that the only hope for a shorter approach was from Churchill Fort to the east end of the lake. In 1792, Turnor explored the Nelson River up to the mouth of the Burntwood River. There he learned from the Indians that a small portage crossed from the Burntwood to the Churchill River. Turnor departed by ship the same year for London where he set his information and views before the Committee.

While the representatives of the Hudson's Bay Company still sought a satisfactory route to the riches of the Athabasca, Roderick Mackenzie's newly established post became the point of departure for a still deeper penetration into the interior of northwest America. To Alexander Mackenzie, the fort was a base of operations from which he travelled to the Arctic Ocean in 1789 and to the Pacific in 1793. His explorations would not have been possible without the supplies provided by the new fort. Mackenzie's journeys were the forerunners of the North West Company's exploitation of the Peace River area, the Mackenzie River system, and New Caledonia.[29] The advance of the fur trade into these new frontier regions centred on Fort Chipewyan.

Strategically situated in the heart of a new field abundant in furs, the fort soon became a distribution and communications centre for the North West Company. Fort Chipewyan's role in the North West Company's organization remained of primary importance until the amalgamation of the North West with the Hudson's Bay Company in 1821. Up to that time the fur brigades coming inland stopped at Fort Chipewyan in the autumn to sort and re-pack the goods for their designated districts further north and west. In the spring season, the brigades from these districts, the Peace, Mackenzie and New Caledonia, made *rendez-vous* at the fort. There they packed the furs into the canoes that made up the Athabasca brigade. The fur cargo was transported outward to be exchanged for the next season's outfit of trade goods.

The brigades necessarily employed a considerable number of men for service as voyageurs. This extra complement of men was kept at Fort Chipewyan throughout the winter.

Reports of the activities of the posts to the west and north came in during the winter season. The significant happenings of the district were recorded in the annual winter express, the first of which left Fort Chipewyan in October of 1798 for Sault Ste. Marie.[30] A senior trader superintended the activities of the post and district. In fact, there were often two or three senior partners in residence, especially during the years of competition, so important was this district.

The coming and going of the brigades and the large number of employees usually kept at the fort made a reliable source of provisions imperative. The fisheries normally yielded a steady supply of whitefish and northern pike. Seasonal weather conditions often made fishing impossible, however, meaning an abundance of fish did not always guarantee an adequate food supply. These fisheries meant food or famine to the life of the fort, and had they ever failed, the continued existence of Fort Chipewyan would have been very much in doubt. The Athabasca delta, low, flat and marshy, was a haven for the ducks, geese, and swans that supplemented the daily ration of fish. Moose, deer, and buffalo, although less than plentiful, gave occasional variety to the menu.

Fresh rations of fish and meat, however, were not the provisions that sustained the human engines of the brigades making the long annual voyage from the Athabasca. In the short season of open water, these brigades had no time to collect provisions by fishing and hunting as they travelled; great quantities of dried meat and pemmican were required to assure the brigades would reach their destination. These dried provisions were collected at Fort Chipewyan from the Athabasca and Peace River regions in preparation for the outward journey.

Philip Turnor recorded the North West Company's achievements in the Athabasca. He felt that the Hudson's Bay Company would not make any great gains until it adopted the Canadians' methods.[31] While the Northwesters seemed to proceed from success to success in the Athabasca, the Company on the Bay faced a number of urgent problems in the early 1790s: the need to expand up the Saskatchewan; the encroachment of the Montrealers in the "Muskrat Country"; the decline of trade at Churchill; and the approach to the Athabasca still remained uncertain.[32] For an effective solution to these problems the Hudson's Bay Company required not only more manpower, but undivided leadership; both of these were lacking in 1793. The outbreak of war in Europe in that year caused a manpower shortage that seriously affected the Company's trade in America for the next twenty years.[33] The conflict between Joseph Colen at York and William Tomison at Cumberland weakened the Hudson's Bay Company's organization in North America.[34] Tomison did not accept Turnor's opinion that the Athabasca was the centre of the opposition; he was intent on organizing a profitable trade on the Saskatchewan.[35] Colen seemed more concerned with rebuilding York's trade in the hinterland of the Bay.[36] The activities of the North West Company began seriously to diminish the English company's returns in this region. William McGillivray's opposition from 1787 to 1790 in the vicinity of Reindeer Lake proved particularly effective.[37]

Convinced by Turnor of the importance of the Athabasca expedition, the Committee appointed Malchom Ross "Master of the Northward" in 1793.[38] Ross, who had accompanied Turnor on his Athabasca survey, also believed there was a shorter route to the Athabasca than that through Cumberland House. The journey to the Athabasca by way of Cumberland House on the Saskatchewan involved an extra thousand miles from York and Churchill on the Bay. A short cut could give the Bay men a chance to reach the Athabasca before their rivals each season, a distinct advantage in equipping the Indians with fall outfits. Ross hoped that he would be fortunate enough to find natives who knew and possibly travelled the short cut, just as Pond's fortune had been in finding the guides who knew the Portage La Loche approach to the far northwest. Ross drowned in 1799 while continuing his search for an alternate route to the Athabasca.

David Thompson, Ross's colleague in the search for a

northward approach, succeeded in reaching the east end of Lake Athabasca in July, 1796.[39] Setting out in 1794 from York, Ross and Thompson travelled up the Nelson-Burntwood rivers and crossed the portage to the Churchill River where they wintered at Fairford House[40] in 1795-96. In the spring of 1796, Thompson, in company with two Chipewyan guides, made his way up Reindeer River, through Reindeer Lake, and over the Cochrane River to Wollaston Lake from where he proceeded down the Black River to Lake Athabasca. Thompson and Ross spent the next year in a vain attempt to reach the Athabasca by the same path. The lack of deep water and provisions proved to be obstacles in the way of this approach.[41] With Thompson's resignation from the Hudson's Bay Company in 1797 and Ross's untimely death in 1799, the hopes for a northern approach faded.

The Committee took a step in a positive direction by sending orders to York and Churchill in 1799 for the former to withdraw from any Athabasca projects. Churchill was to receive reinforcements for an Athabasca approach. William Linklater set up a trading post at Ile-à-la-Crosse in 1799 while William Auld built Essex House at Green Lake and Peter Fidler built Bolsover House on Meadow Lake. In the same year Fidler also built Greenwich House on Lac la Biche. During the winter he travelled the Lac la Biche River and went up the Athabasca to the mouth of the Lesser Slave Lake River.[42] The extension of the Company's trade into the regions bordering the Athabasca country foreshadowed Fidler's expedition there.

After an unsuccessful venture at Chesterfield House on the South Saskatchewan in 1800, Fidler returned to Cumberland House to prepare for the Athabasca. In 1802, he travelled over the Churchill-Methy-Clearwater route to Lake Athabasca. There, on English Island, he built Nottingham House.[43]

Fidler's attempts at trade epitomized the cautious policy of his employers; the Bay men were hired to trade, not to fight.

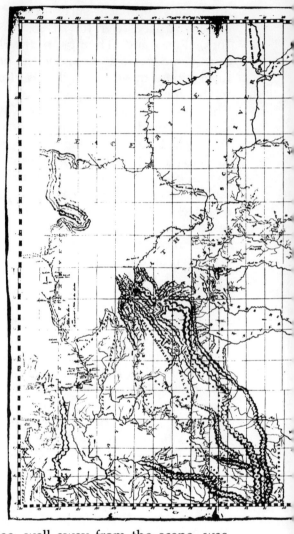

The London Committee, well away from the scene, was guided by a desire not to become embroiled in a test of strength with their Canadian rivals. The object of the Adventurers was not to out-trade their Montreal competitors, but to gain a fair share of the trade to assure a respectable return on their investments:

The great and first object of our Concerns is an Increasing

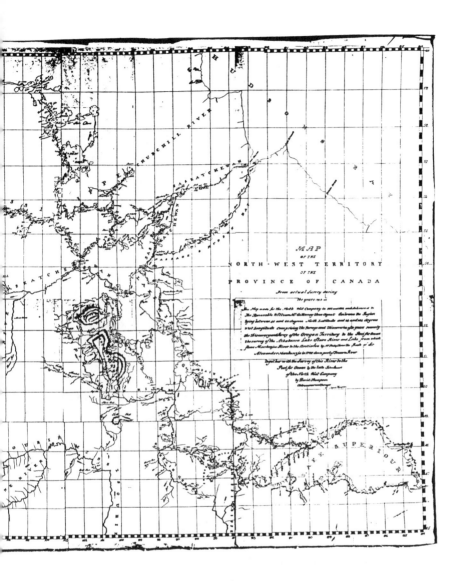

David Thompson's 1813-14 map of the western interior was a notable achievement. The map's accuracy reflects his many voyages of exploration. (Public Archives of Canada, National Map Collection, HI/701/1813-14)

Trade to counterbalance the very enormous and increasing Expenses of it. We do not expect returns equal to those of our more powerful Opponents but we ought to receive such returns as are adequate to the quantity of goods you are annually supplied with.[44]

Fidler's Athabasca campaign was doomed to failure: the Bay men were no match for the aggressive Northwesters. In 1802-03 Fidler and his colleagues spent most of their waking hours seeking sufficient provisions. Thomas Swain was sent to establish a post on Peace River, but he returned during the winter in a near-starved condition, the Canadians having made short work of him. The following season Fidler returned to Nottingham House and once again spent a dismal winter warding off his fierce rivals. In 1805-06, the Bay men spent most of the season confined to their post, overwhelmed by the bullying practices of their Canadian tormentors. Four seasons produced few returns. The Indians were not impressed by the men of Nottingham House. The Hudson's Bay Company abandoned the Athabasca to the North West Company.

The North West Company did not come through this period without suffering internal dissension and the competition of other Canadians in the Athabasca. The surrender of the western posts in 1796 to the United States in accordance with the Jay Treaty of 1794 influenced firms that had been trading in American territory to turn to trading ventures in the British northwest.[45] The XY Company, which had its beginnings in 1798, reached the Athabasca in the following year.[46] The new company approached the Athabasca down the Pembina and Athabasca rivers to Lake Athabasca where it established a post on Little Island.[47] Their Canadian rivals posed a more serious threat than the English to the North West Company's trading organization. The XY Company used similar business methods in extending its inland trade.[48] In 1801, Alexander Mackenzie placed his experience and influence at the head of the firm.[49] In 1802 it was reported that the new competition had a capital equal to that of the North West Company.[50] In the Athabasca country the XY men established posts on Peace River which assured them a supply of provisions for the trade.[51]

Although the XY did not succeed in wresting trade from the older company, the ensuing rivalry marked the beginning of a new spirit of relations for the trade:

> The domestic feud between the old North West Company and the New North West, the XY Company, as it came to be called, habituated the men of both parties to deeds of violence.[52]

Simon McTavish, one of the founders of the North West Company, had a strong personality as evidenced by his nickname, "The Marquis." (Public Archives of Canada, C-164)

Violence came to a climax with the murder of a North West servant by an employee of the XY Company at Fort de l'Isle on the North Saskatchewan in 1802.[53] The outcome of the violence was the Canada Jurisdiction Act of 1803. This act empowered the Governor or Lieutenant-Governor of Lower Canada to appoint Justices of the Peace for the Indian territories. These men could make arrests and commit the parties to trial in Lower Canada. A number of Northwesters were appointed Justices, and they attempted to remove their opposition "under pretense of legal formalities."[54] Simon McTavish's death opened the way for a union of the Canadian companies in 1804, as he had been the focal point of the animosity between the two rival factions.

The North West Company's success in the early nineteenth century aided its plans to expand its trading empire.[55] The proposed projects, finding an acceptable route to the Pacific and organizing a maritime trade, required a great deal of initiative and capital. The Athabasca district was not only to serve as a launching place for the inland expansion to the Pacific, but to supply the furs to finance this expansion as well. The extension of inland trade was bringing increased transportation expenses. Two of the Northwesters, Duncan McGillivray and Alexander Mackenzie, firmly believed these costs could be reduced if the Canadians could obtain a right of transit through Hudson Bay.[56]

Although undismayed by the 1804 Canadian coalition, the Hudson's Bay Company, aware of the legal opinion that its Charter was not based on parliamentary sanction but solely on royal prerogative, and aware also that it could not afford a trade war with its rivals, decided to seek a settlement at the bargaining table.[57] The Northwesters were also quite prepared to negotiate an agreement. The Committee was willing either to enter a union with the North West Company or to sell its assets and properties to the Company.[58] The negotiations broke off in 1806 when neither party could agree upon whether the centre of trade should be in London or Montreal, and when a guarantee that would have seen all Canadian traders adhere to a negotiated settlement failed.[59]

Since the turn of the century the Hudson's Bay Company had faced rising costs and lower prices caused by the Napoleonic wars and unsettled conditions in Europe. Its dividend fell from 8 percent to 4 percent in 1801. From 1806 to 1808 the furs piled up in the warehouses with no chance for export.[60] In 1809, no dividend was paid. With a lack of both markets and recruits, the Committee despaired of continuing in the fur trade business.[61] Only the entry of Andrew Wedderburn onto the Committee prevented the Company from temporarily withdrawing from the trade. Wedderburn, John Halkett, and Thomas Douglas, the Earl of Selkirk, brought with them a business initiative that changed the course of the Hudson's Bay Company's policy.[62]

The Retrenching Plan, as Wedderburn's plan came to be called, rested upon a firm commitment to continue in the fur trade.[63] The firm was to stabilize its position in the trade through sound and economical management. There was to be a profit-sharing plan with the servants of the Company. The rest of the plan came from the suggestions of William Auld and Colin Robertson.

William Auld had been interested in gaining a foothold in the Athabasca for a number of years.[64] He believed the approach to the Athabasca must come from Churchill. In 1807, Fidler had travelled inland from Churchill toward Lake Athabasca on what was reported to be a new track.[65] Auld spent the winter of 1808 at Reindeer Lake where he became convinced of the necessity of an Athabasca campaign led by men who would be willing to use force against the Northwesters. His conviction rings in his emphatic comment, "Good God! See the Canadians come thousands of miles beyond us to monopolize the most valuable part of your Territories."[66] It was at Reindeer Lake that Auld met the Northwester Colin Robertson, who, dissatisfied with his present employers, decided on a change. Robertson's ideas on trade matched Auld's. Both men travelled to London in 1809 to lay their views before the Committee. The instructions subsequently given acknowledged the necessity for more active servants who would at least defend themselves and their employer's property:

> We expect that you will defend like men the property that
> is entrusted to you; and if any person shall presume to make
> a forcible attack on you, you have arms in your hands and
> the Law sanctions you in using them for your own defence.[67]

An Athabasca enterprise was, moreover, recognized to be
an important part of any further trade activity:

> [A]s the discussions of 1814 and 1815 emerged . . . it became
> more and more clear that an Athabasca venture was accepted
> as the decisive issue.[68]

The Hudson's Bay Company prepared to undertake the
Athabasca campaign in 1814 by engaging Colin Robertson
to recruit and outfit an expedition in Montreal for the
Athabasca country. In 1815, John Clarke travelled to the
Athabasca by the Methy-Clearwater route. He built Fort
Wedderburn on Potato Island. The North West Company
was now opposed by men who knew how to counter the
methods of the 'Northwest spirit.' Undaunted by a disastrous
year, Clarke returned in 1816, only to find a tougher
opposition. A prisoner until August, 1817, Clarke was unable
to form an 1817-18 outfit; the Bay men only placed a token
force on the lake that season. Colin Robertson led the 1818-19
brigade into Athabasca and the season proved to be more
successful. The determination of the Bay men to return each
succeeding season began to make an impression on the
Indians. Robertson correctly believed that the first goal
should be to win them over; the furs would follow.

Relations between the two rival companies throughout the
northwest had deteriorated to such a degree that trade was
interrupted and violence not unknown. The North West
Company wintering partners were becoming increasingly
dissatisfied with the uncertain conditions under which they
operated, and as a result were not averse to a merger
proposal. As well, the North West Company did not have
the financial resources to withstand concerted opposition.
By 1821 a deal was struck, and the two companies

amalgamated under the name of the Hudson's Bay Company.

The Athabasca conflict was over. The necessity of adapting fur trade practices to the new monopoly was now the order of the day.

Colin Robertson, who left the North West Company for the Hudson's Bay Company, persuaded the London Committee to compete for the Athabasca trade. (Public Archives of Canada, C-8984)

2. THE FORTS: THEIR LOCATIONS AND STRUCTURES

A. Locations

The discovery of an approach to the Athabasca country was the first step in organizing the area as a fur trade district. The next step involved identifying suitable sites for trading posts. While the demand for furs was the driving force behind the expansion of the inland trade, other important factors determined the choice of a fort site. While some factors affected the location of most forts, such as its proximity to Indian bands and to water routes for transportation, specific factors often assumed greater significance at individual forts. At Fort Chipewyan, the traders had to take into account the confluence of three major river systems, a large delta, and Lakes Athabasca and Claire. The position of ice in the fall and the ensuing spring breakup when currents were reversed complicated the choice of location. The problem of transportation in the immediate vicinity of the fort was of critical importance at Fort Chipewyan.

Even if all these conditions were successfully overcome, unexpected developments could force the relocation or abandonment of a fort. With no knowledge of where the Indians lived or of possible sources of provisions, the first traders had to depend on native advice and their own experience.[1] As well, in the years preceding 1821, the entry of rival traders into a district could force an existing post to change location. Finally, the posts generally tended to move deeper into the heart of a region as the fur trade developed there. The Athabasca district did not escape these challenges as a succession of traders sought to make it a profitable fur trading region.

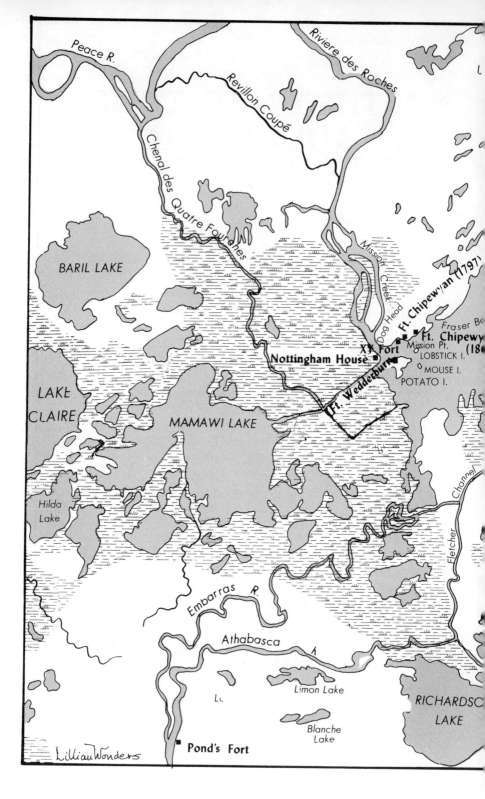

Peace R.

Riviere des Roches

Revillon Coupé

Chenal des Quatre Fourches

BARIL LAKE

Mission Creek

Dog Head

Ft. Chipewyan (1791)

Fraser B

Ft. Chipewy

(18

Mission Pt.

XX Fort

LOBSTICK I.

Nottingham House

MOUSE I.

POTATO I.

LAKE
CLAIRE

Ft. Wedderburn

MAMAWI LAKE

Hilda
Lake

Fletcher Channel

Embarras R.

Athabasca

Limon Lake

RICHARDSO
LAKE

Blanche
Lake

Lillian Wonders

■ **Pond's Fort**

26

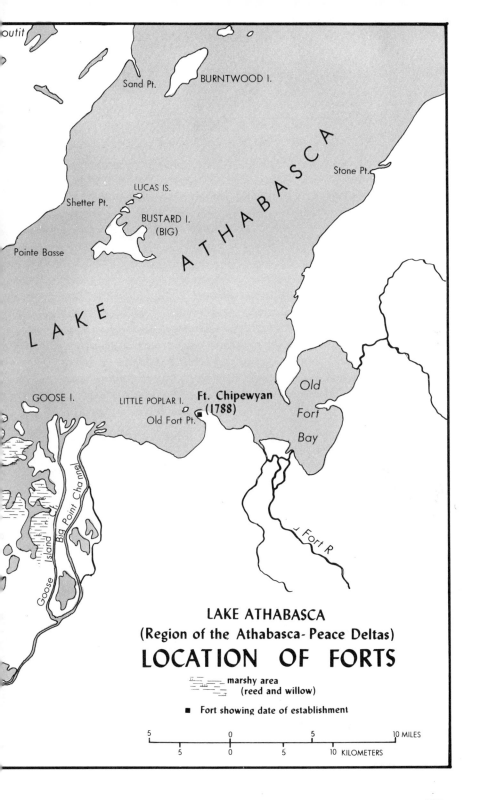

outit

Sand Pt.

BURNTWOOD I.

LAKE ATHABASCA

Stone Pt.

LUCAS IS.

Shetter Pt.

BUSTARD I.
(BIG)

Pointe Basse

LAKE

GOOSE I.

LITTLE POPLAR I.

Ft. Chipewyan
(1788)

Old Fort Pt.

Old
Fort
Bay

Big Point Channel

Goose Island

J. Fort R

LAKE ATHABASCA
(Region of the Athabasca- Peace Deltas)
LOCATION OF FORTS

marshy area
(reed and willow)

■ Fort showing date of establishment

5   0   5   10 MILES

5   0   5   10 KILOMETERS

27

In 1778, Peter Pond made a successful approach over the Portage La Loche and down the Clearwater and Athabasca rivers to a spot approximately forty miles south of the lake. There, on the east bank of the Athabasca River, about half a mile past the point where the Embarras River branches off, he built a trading house. The site was noted in 1791 by the Hudson's Bay Company surveyor, Philip Turnor:

> the river at this place parts into two branches followed the Eastern one, the river passed this day much as before, went in the East branch N ½ and came to Peter Ponds [sic] old House. . . .[2]

Guy Blanchet, a Dominion Lands Surveyor, said that the fort was located near the cutbank where the Embarras branches from the main current, although he could find nothing of the original site.[3] Snowbird Marten, an old trapper who has lived near the entrance of the Embarras all his life, said that a number of old graves upstream had been washed into the river.[4] The erosion is quite heavy along the shore and it is possible that the original site has been washed away.

In the choice of a site, Pond was undoubtedly influenced by three considerations: the availability of a food supply, the proximity of a water route, and the prospects for trade. Adequate provisions were a necessity for survival through the long winter months. The banks of the Athabasca River sheltered moose and deer, assuring Pond of a food supply. Big game would probably be scarce on the delta that stretched north from the trading house. The rations of the traders were supplemented by the produce from a garden Pond planted.[5] With scant knowledge of the delta and lake, Pond probably preferred to remain on the river where he knew he could leave soon after the break-up. His experience would tell him the ice on the river would go out before that on the lake. Then too, the spring voyage would be upstream to the Portage La Loche, and the necessity of tracking the canoes for a great part of the way was probably taken into consideration.[6] Furthermore, Pond may not have had guides who knew the intricate routes leading to and from the lake. The Athabasca delta is a maze of creeks and rivers, bewildering to all but the most experienced voyageur.

Pond could also have been trying to locate his fort nearer the territory of the Crees than that of the Chipewyans to ensure close access to interpreters whom he and his men could understand. Pond and his men were certainly able to communicate in Cree and it is perhaps significant that his fort was located near the northernmost edge of the Cree country. Were he to winter in the Chipewyan and Beaver country, he might experience difficulty in gathering provisions from the Crees as the tribes were not on the friendliest terms in the latter part of the eighteenth century.[7] The Chipewyans were never noted for their generosity in trading provisions.[8] A letter from Alexander Henry the Elder to Joseph Banks in 1781 on the possibility of a route to the Pacific through the Athabasca country hinted at the language problem:

> when everything is ready and provisions procured for the summer, as no dependance can be put, on what you are to receive in an unknown part. . . . A new sett of interpretors and guides must be procured. . . .[9]

Henry did not travel beyond Ile-à-la-Crosse Lake and his account of the country beyond the headwaters of the Churchill River was undoubtedly based on information from Pond.[10]

Finally, Pond chose a location where the Indians could be intercepted when they travelled out with their furs to Ile-à-la-Crosse, Cumberland House, and Hudson Bay. The trade route followed the Churchill River, and the only means of reaching the Churchill was by travelling up the Athabasca and Clearwater rivers.[11] The best possible point at which to intercept the brigades, then, was where the Athabasca River flows into the delta. It branches into two main channels near Pond's house; the Embarras River meanders in a northerly direction, and the main channel makes an easterly swing before flowing into the lake.

Pond's buildings are unfortunately not described in any surviving documents; the only hint comes from Alexander

Mackenzie who described Pond's first residence as a "tent" on the river bank.[12] There must have been some kind of dwelling for the twenty men who accompanied Pond. This fort remained the fur trade *rendez-vous* for the next decade.[13]

From this post on the Athabasca River, the fur traders pushed west and north into the Peace and Great Slave regions. Apparently Pond did not have too much time for exploration in the Athabasca until his third trip into the country in 1783 when he went in early from Ile-à-la-Crosse. It is possible that he also explored Lake Athabasca. He learned of a river leading to an ocean from Indians who had accompanied Hearne on his Coppermine expedition.[14] These initial explorations led to trading expeditions. In 1786, Cuthbert Grant and Laurent Leroux established rival posts on Great Slave Lake.[15] In November, Alexander McLeod and Charles Boyer set out on foot for Peace River with twelve men and nine hundred pounds of goods and returned to the fort in December of the same year.[16] The briefness of their journey meant they did not penetrate any great distance into the Peace River region. The failure of the canoes to reach Pond's house before freeze-up in 1787 led Alexander Mackenzie to report in 1788 that the prospects for trade were discouraging unless a place could be established which would attract the Chipewyans. He thought there was little chance of getting goods to Peace River and Great Slave Lake before freeze-up. The outlook would be improved if a *rendez-vous* could be established near Lake Athabasca in Chipewyan country.[17]

Alexander Mackenzie's ambitious plans for an extension of the fur trade, coupled with his idea of reaching the Pacific Ocean, were sufficient to gain the support of his cousin, Roderick Mackenzie. In 1788 Roderick accompanied Alexander to Pond's fort where the outfits were made up for the Athabasca. Roderick then travelled north to the lake. In his words:

> I looked out for a suitable spot for a new establishment to replace the old one of Mr. Pond. After making every possible inquiry and taking every measure of precaution I pitched

on a conspicuous projection that advances about a league into the Lake, the base of which appeared in the shape of a person sitting with her arms extended, the palms forming as if it were a point.[18]

The point of land referred to projects into the lake about six miles east of the river's east branch, now Big Point Channel. The land (marked on maps as Old Fort Point and hereafter referred to as such) extends well into the lake, evidence of Mackenzie's "every measure of precaution." The site was surrounded by water on three sides; the only approach by land was from the south. The fort was built on the west side of the point, where it was sheltered from the east winds blowing off the lake. The route of the canoes to the main channel was protected by islands and bays along the south shore. Certainly the south shore provided more timber growth for a wood supply than the scrub growth on the north shore.[19] The bush and forest on the south shore was also a better habitat of moose and deer than the north shore. Big game, however, was not so much in Mackenzie's thoughts as the availability of fisheries:

> It [the fort site] is altogether a beautiful, healthy situation, in the center of many excellent and never-failing fisheries, provided they are duly attended to at the proper season.[20]

The fisheries around Old Fort Point provided an abundance of whitefish and pike for the fort's residents. The other fisheries were centred around Goose Island, Little Poplar Island, one half mile north and west of the fort, and Bustard Island, which is situated approximately eight miles across the lake.

Although the south shore site had many advantages, the expansion of the trade made relocation of the fort necessary. Alexander Mackenzie's explorations revealed the opportunity for the expansion of the trade beyond Lake Athabasca. In order to exploit this potential the canoes had to reach the Peace River country and Great Slave Lake before freeze-up. No doubt Roderick Mackenzie explored every possibility when the need became evident.[21]

The traders' interest in setting up trading posts on the northwest shore arose from several factors. The need for a *rendez-vous* had been to provide a depot for the developing trade of the Peace and Mackenzie regions. Hence, as the trade was extended, the northwest shore proved to be a more central location than Old Fort Point. Although the main channels of the Athabasca River entered the lake near Old Fort Point, the Embarras River and smaller streams flowed in a more northerly direction to the west end of the lake. These latter streams were usually the first free of ice in the delta. The early opening of the channel on the northwest shore proved to be a major consideration.

The northwest shore forts were situated in the channel of water that led from Lake Athabasca. Around Dog Head, the Rivière des Rocher ran almost due north for some thirty miles, where it met the Peace River.[22] South of the entrance to the Rivière des Rocher the Chenal des Quatre Fourches flowed four miles west to a junction with streams from the south and west (hence its name, Four Forks). The west channel connected with Mamawi and Claire lakes. The main channel of the Quatre Fourches wound north approximately forty miles, to join the Peace River. The Rocher and Quatre Fourches rivers normally drained Lake Athabasca except when the Peace River was in flood in the spring and early summer. It was then that these two channels carried the overflow of the Peace River into the lake. Thus, the current of the channel by the northwest shore was reversed until the water level of the lake was brought up by the spring floods of the Athabasca River. The Athabasca River usually broke up after the Peace in the vicinity of the lake since the delta of the former slowed the force of the spring run-off.

The time of the break-up was undoubtedly a factor in relocation. At Old Fort Point the ice did not break as soon as the ice on the northwest shore channel. The ice of this channel was broken up by the reversal of the current. The problem of the ice was noted in April of 1792 by Philip Turnor:

> began to haul the Furrs &c to within about 6½ miles of the

mouth of the Athapescow river to be in readiness to proceed up the river so soon as it is clear of ice . . . if we had remained at the House in expectation of going out of the Lake at water we might have been detained many days by the wind setting the Ice from the Westward in upon this shore. . . .[23]

The Northwesters must have encountered difficulty in getting the furs away in the spring before Turnor's visit. The ice would not only be pushed against Old Fort Point by a west wind, but also by an east wind which, coming down the lake, tended to force the drift ice against the south shore.

Two other factors intensified the need for open water routes in early spring. The provisions needed by outgoing brigades came from the Peace River country. The reversing of the current meant that the provisions and furs could be delivered to the *rendez-vous* quite early. Then too, Great Slave-Mackenzie River canoes could easily reach a northwest site. From the northwest shore, the first open water route to the south was through the Embarras River and its tributaries.

The location of the Indians also influenced the choice of a site. Roderick Mackenzie probably found that the south shore site, although situated near abundant fisheries, and with a beautiful view, was not the best place for meeting the Chipewyans. Their lands lay to the north and east of Fort Chipewyan and, as they were not adept in the handling of canoes, they experienced considerable difficulty in crossing the lake in summer. Wind conditions also make the lake dangerous to cross at this point. Cuthbert Grant (senior) most likely realized this problem when he set up his post on the north shore, near what today is called Fidler Point. He established this post "at the principal pass of the Caribou Eaters, when they were coming to this place."[24] The desire to build a fort for trade with the Chipewyans must have been considered in relocation because the south shore site was closer to Cree territory than Chipewyan territory. The hostility of the two tribes also had to be taken into consideration.

The exact date of the change in sites is unknown. It has been set around 1804 but this date is rather late.[25] It becomes obvious from Peter Fidler's Nottingham House Journals that the North West Company was already located on the north shore by this time. It took Fidler four and a half hours to sail and paddle across the lake to the "French houses." The Indians had already assembled at Fort Chipewyan to await their fall advances.[26] A careful study of James Mackenzie's 1799-1800 journal leads to the conclusion that the fort had been established on the north shore for some time. Mackenzie referred to several places, such as the Pointe aux Chiens (Dog Head), that are on the north shore. Mackenzie also complained of the poor condition of the fort: the pickets were falling down, and the bark covering was rotten.[27] It is obvious then, that the fort had been located on the north shore for some time. The state of the buildings suggests at least two or three years, placing the move in 1796 or 1797.

The North West Company's first fort on the northwest shore was situated near or on what is now called Mission Point. Fidler records that Nottingham House (on English Island) was located about three-quarters of a mile from Fort Chipewyan.[28] The most logical place at this distance is Mission Point which gives an excellent view of the lake in every direction.

The arrival of competition at the close of the century brought about a further change in sites. On 22 May 1800, James Mackenzie records the arrival of three opposition canoes at Bustard Island.[29] A.S. Morton stated that six more canoes went in by way of the Pembina River from the Saskatchewan.[30] Although Mackenzie did not mention the arrival of more canoes, it is possible that more arrived since his journal ends on 5 September. Perronne, the opposition trader, was attempting to get to Ile-à-la-Crosse, no doubt with the intention of supplying provisions to incoming canoes and to act as a guide.[31] James Mackenzie's reaction to competitors was, "In order to prevent them from building a fort on the Pointe au Sable the prettiest spot for that purpose on this side of the Lake Mr. Finlay marked it for the N W Co."[32] The XY company chose Little Island, directly in front of Fort Chipewyan on Mission Point.[33]

When Peter Fidler arrived in 1802 then, the fur posts of the Canadian companies were already situated on the northwest shore. Fidler chose a site on the southeast corner of English Island where there was an adequate wood supply and a fishery close at hand.[34] Having dispatched Thomas Swain with nine men in three canoes for Peace River, Fidler and the seven men remaining commenced building a trading house, 50' by 15'. In addition to the main house, men's houses were built. The roofs and walls were mudded in and the interior walls were whitewashed.[35] They constructed a fish storage shed in December. A garden that yielded turnips and potatoes was planted in 1803, and a seven-foot stockade was built around it in 1805.[36] In October of 1803, the Northwesters built a watch house close by Nottingham House.

As a result of this competition, in 1803 the North West Company moved to what became the permanent site of Fort Chipewyan.[37] The move was very likely occasioned by the fact that the XY fort on Little Island was in a better position to intercept the Indians coming in from the east. The XY men promptly moved their house to a place near Fort Chipewyan.[38] After the North West Company had moved, Fidler planned to relocate his house as well. His men cut logs for a house with the dimensions of 50' by 17' by 14'. The move never came about, no doubt because servants were in short supply the following year.[39]

After the coalition of the Canadian companies in 1804, the full brunt of competition fell upon the small force of Bay men. Intimidated by the North West "bullies," and with nothing to show in fur returns, the Hudson's Bay Company relinquished its precarious hold on the Athabasca country in 1806.[40]

When the Company returned to the Athabasca in 1815, John Clarke began the construction of Fort Wedderburn on Potato

Island, immediately across the channel from the North West Company headquarters at Fort Chipewyan. The site proved unsuitable because of its proximity to the belligerent North West men.[41] The Company rebuilt the fort on the other (the northwest) side of the island.[42] In May of 1821, George Simpson reported the buildings to be "scarcely habitable," and felt it would be necessary to "erect a Dwelling House this Summer."[43] Despite Fort Chipewyan's noted inadequacies, Simpson found it "a magnificent Establishment compared with this," a good indication of the sorry state of the Company's fort.

After the amalgamation of 1821, Fort Chipewyan became the new Company's headquarters in the Athabasca district. Its superior location and better facilities had ensured its selection. Fort Wedderburn was simply abandoned.

In the Athabasca district, the posts were gradually moved north from Pond's House on the Athabasca River to a final location on the northwest shore of the lake. The various companies made each move deliberately, whether in response to the activities of rival traders, or to the need for better access to transportation routes. As the traders became more familiar with a new district, the best location for a fort to meet its fur trading as well as provisioning requirements became clearer. The traders operating in Athabasca were no different, and they responded as best they could to the conditions in their district.

B. Structures

The specific information available about the various forts' buildings is incomplete. Additional information can be inferred from comparison with other period data.

Unfortunately, no account of the south shore fort appears to have survived. In 1791, however, Malchom Ross noted the size of the buildings constructed for the Turnor-Ross expedition:

> Employed laying the foundation of the house which is 24 feet long by 15 feet wide, standing East and West; this is for

Mr. Turnor and the rest of the people. Viz: - 10 foot partitioned off at the west end for Mr. Turnor, the remainder for the people. I also had another separate place 18 foot by 15 and stands N & south, with a door to the Westward - this latter place is for myself, a little goods, and provisions if I get any - 7 foot at the north and divided off for the warehouse or trading room.[44]

The earliest surviving description of Fort Chipewyan is in James Mackenzie's 1799 journal. The fort had by then been relocated to the north shore. The number of buildings and their size cannot be determined. Mackenzie's account is rather querulous as he compares Fort Chipewyan to Mr. McLeod's fort at the forks of the Peace River:

> At Mr. McLeod's fort, the men's houses are better arranged than the Bourgeois' houses here. The fort is built with 5 Bastions; Courtyards are made everywhere, a spacious garden made around the fort, a well, a powder House and even a S____ House are made in this Garden. Here we have neither of these Conveniences - nor do we want any of them except the two most necessary vist . . . a powder House and Hangard . . . we don't presume to find fault with the Gentlemen who arranged Peace River fort . . . but we do for leaving this for of greater Consequence so ill arranged. . . .[45]

From this comparision, it appears that Fort Chipewyan did not have bastions, courtyards, gardens, a well, or a powder magazine in 1799. The condition of the fort is revealed in Mackenzie's facetious remarks that the occupants were "in imminent danger of being squeezed to death by the fort Picketts [sic]" since "some were flat on the ground and several more are in doubt whether they should fall or not."[46] He complained that one could easily thrust a hand through the bark covering the hangards (warehouses) and the locks could be picked by a child. The occasion for Mackenzie's outburst had been provided by sparks from one of the men's houses nearly setting fire to the roof of the warehouse that housed the ammunition.[47]

The condition of this first fort on the north shore indicates that it was poorly planned and constructed. A possible reason may have been that the entry of competition into the Athabasca necessitated a hasty relocation of the fort.

The buildings were never of the best construction, however, especially in the early years of Fort Chipewyan. Fort buildings usually had to be hastily constructed, and often received little maintenance if other activities were more pressing. Many Canadian forts used the *poteaux sur sole* method of construction familiar to the French Canadians who built them. In this type of construction, a framework of squared posts was first set up. These posts had grooves (known as tenons) cut in them to accommodate the squared logs. The logs had ends (mortices) cut to fit the grooves in the posts. Additional posts were placed for doorways and windows. At the centre of the end of each building a post extended to the height of the roof. A ridge pole was then laid on these two end posts and slab timbers were laid from the ridge pole to the eaves for the roof.[48]

References

1. Front Gate
2. Flag Staff
3. Rocking Press
4. Stores with Ice Cellars
5. Pond's Magazine Yard
6. Interpreter and Guides House
7. Ft. Chipewyan Summer & Winter House
8. Covered Passage
9. Watch House Observatory
10. Depot Summer House
11. Depot Summer House Kitchen
12. Depot Summer House Fish Oven
13. Lookout
14. Winter Fish Oven
15. Ft. Chipewyan Kitchen
16. Men's Houses & Blacksmith Shop
17. Black Houses or Bastions
18. Summer Court & Woodyard
19. Winter Court & Woodyard
20. Side Gate

1 Boat Store
1 Canoe Store   } in yard
1 Stable
1 Dogs Kennel Yard   } Are within the Fort

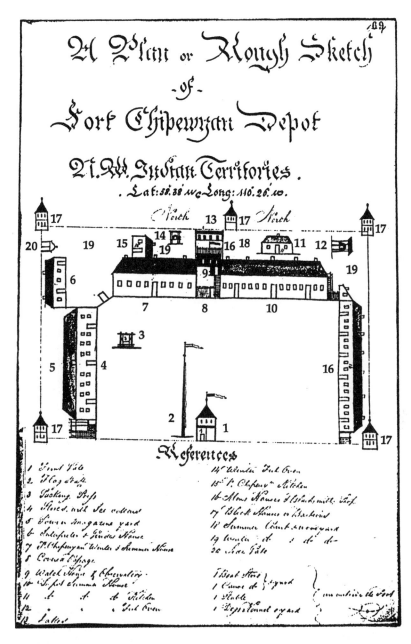

"A Plan or Rough Sketch of Fort Chipewyan Depot," by James Keith, 1823. (Hudson's Bay Company Archives, Provincial Archives of Manitoba)

James Keith gave the best description of Fort Chipewyan in 1823.[49] His drawing shows the various houses joined together in the traditional manner of contemporary fort buildings. Of these buildings, the summer and winter house (#7), and the summer house depot would be the most important because they housed the officers and the trade goods. The summer and winter house contained the assembly hall which Henry Lefroy described in 1843 as being "the greatest feature of the houses in this country. Here the Indians assemble when at the fort, and here they live and sleep."[50]

Unfortunately, Keith did not give any idea of the size of the buildings. William Brown, however, did provide a graphic word description of Fort Wedderburn, which, from a recent survey of both sites, must have had approximately the dimensions of Fort Chipewyan.[51] At Fort Wedderburn, the officer's house was 43' by 22', and divided into a 12' by 22' master's room, a 21' by 22' hall, and two cabins, each 10' by 11'. These cabins were probably used by clerks. Brown mentioned that plans were being made to build another house to replace this of the dimensions 86' by 24'. The store at Wedderburn, 57' by 19', was divided into a 21' by 19' packing store, an 18' by 19' trading room, and a provision store of 18' by 19'. The stores (#4) at Fort Chipewyan held provisions of fish, dried and fresh meat, pemmican, garden produce and trade goods.[52] The men's houses and blacksmith's shop (#16), located on the east wing, probably housed the carpenter's shop. At Fort Wedderburn the men's house, 40' by 18' was "divided by a partition, with a fire place in each division."[53] An older men's quarters had housed the blacksmith's shop. A new building, 36' by 14', contained a carpenter's shop of 16' by 14', and "two rooms of ten feet by fourteen feet each - both of which are well calculated for officers who have families."[54] These measurements indicate the quarters for family living were quite small.

Although Keith's sketch was not drawn to scale, it does display what seem to be a large number of windows in all the main houses. Whether all these windows only existed in the wishful imagination of the artist is not clear. Henry

Lefroy commented on windows in his description of the fort, but this was in 1843, following a period of rebuilding:

> It is a square area, fenced by high palisades, and containing low one-storied buildings on three sides. Nearly all of them display nothing but parchment windows which have particularly cheerless look, as you will imagine if you consider for a moment what it would be like to get all your light through a drumhead. They do in reality give a good deal of light.[55]

Lefroy also mentioned that all the houses, except those of the officers, had parchment. Presumably then, the officers' rooms had glass windows by this time.

George Back, in his description of the house at Fort Reliance in 1833, says that the logs were plastered with a "cement composed of common clay and sand."[56] At Fort Chipewyan, the roofs were plastered with a mixture of clay and grass and sand.[57] Pine bark, gathered by the men in early summer, was used to shingle the dwellings.[58] The pine bark, unlike cedar bark used in the Rainy Lake country,[59] dried out quite readily; hence it was necessary to renew the covering of the houses every year if they were to be reasonably waterproof.[60] Priority was given to the stores and officers' dwellings in

> carting the remainder of the Pine bark up and if we have a sufficiency it is my intention to get the Men's houses covered to protect their property from spoiling from these leaky houses.[61]

William Brown remarked upon the condition of Fort Chipewyan in 1820:

> The buildings originally have been well executed, but they are decaying very fast, and they do not appear to be at much trouble in repairing them.[62]

The run down condition of the fort can be directly attributed to the lack of time during the period of competition to keep the buildings in good repair. After the 1821 amalgamation, however, more time could be allowed for the repair and rebuilding of the fort.[63] New stockades were completed in the summer of 1822. In 1823, the men built a new canoe store and rebuilt the powder magazine.[64] Piecemeal rather than major improvements continued throughout the 1820s, possibly a result of the policy to reduce the number of *engagés* at the fort. In 1824, the factors complained of the want of hands to carry out assignments.[65] Other relics from the days of competition, the bastions that had served as lookouts, were relegated to roles of lesser importance after the amalgamation:

> Four men began to make Bastions as they call them, but not for Defence on the contrary for the Purpose of securing their fish after having been served out to them from the dogs. . . .[66]

In 1828, however, plans were made to begin new buildings.[67] Although some work was carried out,[68] Chief Factor Stewart, on his arrival from York Factory, remarked:

> I must confess the appearance of this place, gave very little proof of much improvement in the summer a circumstance commonly the result of sudden changes of managers.[69]

He subsequently ordered some repairs "in the Fort, which is falling in all directions."[70] The fort remained in need of major repair until the fall of 1832 when Chief Factor John Charles stated at length:

> we began to take part of the summer house, for the north end of it is within a few feet of T. Hodgon's chimney . . . as well as the Fire place of the Blacksmith's forge and when the wind happens to be northeasterly the sparks from the chimneys beat direct against the end of the House . . . intend to take down two rooms from the Old Summer Establishment which will shorten it by 30 feet and leave an open space that will prevent any apprehensions in the future. In short the whole establishment requires renewing, if we could only get it done, but with other Duty that must absolutely be attended to, unless we had more people it is unlikely, that much will be done towards it for some time to come. . . .[71]

Something did get done in the next two years. A 50' by 20'

house was constructed in 1833.[72] The men built a 40' by 20' store in 1832,[73] and had begun another slightly larger one in 1834.[74]

The fort's material comforts often mirrored the condition of the fort itself. The furnishings were barely adequate, especially in the early years. James Mackenzie recorded an indicative accomplishment on 18 August 1799:

> Laviollette finished the Chair - I may be found fault with for employing a man in the Summer to make such a triffling thing as a chair but I cannot help it for I was in want of one and could not write without it.[75]

An entry in the 1823 Fort Chipewyan journal noted that some rooms had been plastered and whitewashed. The journal also reveals that the officers warranted bedsteads, and James Keith had had a writing desk made for himself.[76]

In 1843, Lefroy described his room as twelve feet square, and furnished with a table, chair, and "a rickety old construction of a cupboard made in former days by some luxurious clerk."[77] Furniture was sparse, rough, and usually country-made.

The houses were at least described as being very warm, "the Fires we indulge in would almost warm a barn."[78] Many of the chimneys had double fireplaces, meaning one chimney served two fireplaces in rooms separated by a partition. The chimneys were constructed in much the same manner as the one which David Thompson described at Saleesh House:

> Our Chimneys were made of stone and mud rudely worked in for about six feet in height and eighteen inches thick, the rest of the layers of grass and mud worked around small poles inserted in the stone work, with cross pieces and thus carried up to about four feet above the roof; the fireplace is raised a little, and three to four feet in width by about fifteen inches in depth.[79]

By the time of Lefroy's visit, the buildings could better hold the heat, and certainly more adequate supplies of firewood were collected. Providing firewood fell to the *engagés*, and the quota that a man was required to cut increased from three cords in 1799[80] to twenty-five cords in 1829.[81] The increase in quota is an indication of the increase in the size of the fort.

Fur trade post buildings were utilitarian structures, often hastily constructed with whatever materials and tools were at hand. Furnishings, especially in the earlier stages of a remote fort's existence, were sparse and rough: all hands were needed at more essential tasks aimed at ensuring the fort's survival. From the fragmentary information available, however, a reasonably complete picture of Fort Chipewyan, especially after 1800, can be pieced together. The picture that emerges, although often barren, windswept and cold, also contains the bustle, colour and *joie de vivre* well known in the Canadian fur trade.

3. THE PROBLEMS OF TRANSPORTATION AND PROVISION SUPPLY

Supplied with provisions from the Saskatchewan and aided by not having to return to Grand Portage, Peter Pond succeeded in reaching the Athabasca country in 1778.[1] By returning with 140 fur packs, he proved the Athabasca was worth further efforts to tap its fur reserves.[2] It was tantalizingly reported that he was forced to leave as many more because he lacked the means to bring them out.[3] Also of significance, however, is the fact that he and his men arrived at Cumberland House "in a very distressed state for want of provisions."[4] From the beginning, then, transportation and ensuring an adequate supply of provisions proved to be the major problems affecting the Athabasca trade.[5] The success of the trade at Fort Chipewyan would depend on finding solutions to these problems.

The letters of Alexander Mackenzie suggest that the Canadians were able to maintain only a tenuous hold on the Athabasca in the 1780s, and a contributing factor was the uncertainty of an adequate food supply.[6] The North West Company required a huge supply of provisions for its voyageurs who manned the canoes from Montreal into the distant heart of the fur trade lands. Evidently Pond or Mackenzie discovered that the Peace River country was a valuable source of meat. This could be dried for use by the voyageurs. Pond, however, has been credited with solving the problem of the Athabasca trade by discovering pemmican to be superior to dried meat, although it has been suggested that Henry Kelsey was the first to use pemmican in his travels with the Plains Indians in 1690-92.[7] Innis has noted that Mackenzie associated the making of pemmican with the

Chipewyan Indians.[8] What is certain, though, is that by the late 1780s, it was an accepted fact that a provision trade could and must be carried on with the natives of the Peace River district, and that this undoubtedly involved pemmican. Alexander Mackenzie noted in February of 1788:

> Messrs. [Alexander] McLeod and [Charles] Boyer went off for the latter place [Peace River] on the 9th November, with twelve men and nine pieces, in order to trade some provisions for the canoes in their voyage out in the Spring. . . .[9]

In the same report, Mackenzie states the need of a *rendez-vous* if a satisfactory trade is to be carried on.

Pond's House was too far south to be in the most advantageous location for gathering provisions from the Peace. This meant the main food supply for the men at the fort would be the moose and buffalo meat required for the outgoing brigades. Another cheap source of food had to be found to feed the men who stayed in the district if there was to be any basis for an expansion of the trade in the Athabasca. Fortunately the excellent fishing grounds on Lake Athabasca were to solve some of the difficulties.

By 1787 the traders certainly knew of these fishing grounds on the lake. Roderick Mackenzie states that they were to "depend on our own industry in fishing for a living"[10] at the new establishment of Fort Chipewyan. Fish could therefore be used to feed the Athabasca traders, while the dry provisions went to feed the canoe brigades. Alexander Mackenzie stresses the role that Fort Chipewyan played in providing food for the fur traders:

> Here have I arrived with ninety or an hundred men without any provision for their sustenance; for whatever quantity might have been obtained from the natives during the summer, it could not be more than sufficient for the people despatched to their different posts; and even if there were a casual superfluity, it was absolutely necessary to preserve it untouched, for the demands of the spring. The whole dependence, therefore, of those who remained, was on the

lake, and fishing implements for the means of our support.[11]

The fisheries that sustained Fort Chipewyan were located around Goose and Bustard Islands, and Old Fort Point. During the summer months, fishing tended to be good near the north shore site of Fort Chipewyan, but in the fall a lowering of the water level caused the fish to move to deeper water. After the canoes arrived, usually in September, the men were sent to Goose Island and Old Fort Point to set up the fall fisheries. In early winter, usually just before freeze-up, a fishery was also set up at Bustard Island (then known as Big Island). A good fall fishery meant that enough fish would be taken to maintain the fort until spring, a fact noted by Turnor:

> This Lake has a very fine fishery for about three weeks after the Ice first sets fast in which time as many may be taken as would serve four Months. . . .[12]

Food, as Mackenzie explains, was often in limited supply in the fall and thus the extra men remaining at Fort Chipewyan were sent to the fisheries to maintain themselves. This became the customary policy whenever there was a shortage of food at the fort. In his 1820-21 report, William Brown notes that, before 1812, the Northwesters used "to starve at this place." Consequently,

> They adopted the plan "Of giving every two fishermen from ten to twelve nets, with a certain number of fish which they were to procure in the course of the season - And in order that their provisions might not be destroyed in bringing them to the Fort, two men were appointed to drive eight or ten traineaux" which haul home their fish in the early part of the season and their meat in the latter. So that they not only receive their provisions at the Fort with very little deduction, but are enabled to dispense with the service of a number of their men, who are either sent in company with their Indians to take care of the Furs they procure, or dispersed in small parties to find their own subsistence, until their service are required in the spring.[13]

Two difficulties complicated operating the fisheries: the

length of the freeze-up in the fall, and transporting the fish to the fort. If the fall freeze-up was a long process of alternate freezing and thawing periods, the lake remained impassable by canoe or sledge. In these circumstances the fort was often reduced to a starvation diet.[14] If the nets were set out before the ice was thick enough, they could be lost or damaged in drift ice.[15] Hauling the fish from the fisheries, a distance from eighteen to twenty-one miles up the lake, proved an arduous task. Men, dogs and traineaux were used after the ice could support their weight. The surface of the ice never failed to present drifts, jagged edges, and ice ridges, making the haul long and hazardous. The possibilities of fog or a blinding snow storm presented additional dangers:

> one of the Old Companies men were very near lost yesterday evening from the Island. 2 of his dog sledges loaded with fish are not to be found - he slept in and lost within one mile of their house - but as the drift was so much he was afraid to leave it. . . .[16]

Small evergreens were placed as markers on the trail in the event of bad weather.

The method of taking the fish remained unchanged throughout the nineteenth century. Philip Turnor noted that nets of 360 feet were best, although some of shorter length were used. In winter, one end of the net was fastened to the end of a long pole which passed by means of forked sticks through a hole and under the ice to another hole. There the other end of the net was secured.[17] David Thompson adds that the floats and weights were of wood and stone, with a net mesh of five to six inches used for whitefish.[18] Roderick Mackenzie describes the disagreeable business of handling the nets:

> The fingers and wrists, while occupied in managing the nets and disentangling the fish from the meshes, must be kept constantly immerged to prevent their freezing.[19]

The number of fish which were caught seems prodigious, but the daily allowance probably averaged eight pounds per man,[20] meaning one hundred men would consume eight hundred pounds each day. Assuming the average weight of a whitefish to be from three to four pounds,[21] this many men would require approximately two hundred fish a day. In one season, 1831-32, the fisheries yielded approximately forty-eight thousand fish,[22] while Brown stated that nearly fifty-seven thousand were taken in 1820-21.[23] Turnor noted that whitefish, pike, and perch made up the general catch while a few trout were also taken:

> the white fish turns very soft after the beginning of December the Perch likewise turn poor the Pike continues good. . . .[24]

Trout was valued as a fish that could be dried and used to feed the canoemen. Peter Fidler's men were obliged to use dried fish for their outward voyages in 1803[25] and 1804.[26]

There were two methods of preserving the fish. In the warm months, the perch and trout were split open and dried on willow sticks in the sun. After freeze-up, the fish were frozen in fish storage sheds at the fisheries and then carried to the fort to be placed in an ice cellar.

"Fort Chepewyan - an establishment of the N.W. Co.Y on the Athabasca Lake (North America)" by Captain Back, c. 1825. The fort can be seen at the right. (Public Archives of Canada, C-15251)

The ration of fish was augmented by wild fowl. Geese, ducks, and swans abounded on the delta in both spring and fall. Turnor describes the ease with which they could be brought down:

> they are then killed setting as they come to the sands at the rate of two or three a shot and they keep flying backwards and forwards the whole day as there is not tide to cover the sands. . . .[27]

The men cured the birds with salt brought from the Salt River, located approximately seventy miles north near the Slave River. These salt springs were situated less than fifteen miles west of a short portage from the Slave to the Salt River. George Back described them in 1834:

> on arriving at the proper spot, we filled our five large bags with pure and white salt, in the short space of half an hour. There were not mounds like those seen in 1820; but just at the foot of the hill which bounds the prairie in that quarter, there were three springs, varying in diameter from four to twelve feet, and producing hillocks of salt, from fourteen to thirty inches in height. The streams were dry, but the surface of the clayey soil was covered, to the extent of a few hundred yards towards the plain, with a white crust of saline particles.[28]

Salt from these springs supplied the districts northwest of Cumberland House.[29] It was a strong mixture, but when ground or pounded well, was suitable for its purpose:

> all the salt was used in the North up to that time and for some years afterwards, was taken from these springs, where it was annually shovelled up into sacks for distribution among the various trading posts of the country. It was regarded by the Company's people as perfectly wholesome. It was, however, considered necessary, in order to make it suited for table use, that it should first be passed through a coffee mill or pounded in a piece of dressed leather.[30]

Most forts made an effort to establish a garden. Gardens supplemented the monotonous diet of fish and dried or cured provisions and, if successful, decreased the amount of food the company had to bring into the fur trade country. Horticulture was first attempted with a modest degree of success at Peter Pond's fort on the Athabasca River.[31] This garden was very likely maintained until the change of fort sites in 1788. It is doubtful whether the North West Company had a garden at the south shore fort. Philip Turnor did not mention one in 1791; Roderick Mackenzie, however, remained inland during some of the summers,[32] and he may have attempted gardening. James Mackenzie does not mention gardens in his 1799 journal. Peter Fidler laid out a garden in 1803 on English Island which, in one season, yielded only one bushel of turnips and ten gallons of potatoes from five gallons of seed.[33]

Fidler noted "the sterility of the Ground & the cold climate" as obstacles to successful gardening.[34] During periods of competition gardens were exposed to the additional hazard of wanton destruction.[35] It is questionable whether the Northwesters ever attempted extensive gardening at Fort Chipewyan. Simpson stated they "pay little or no attention to horticulture in this District."[36] He did not say, however, that they neglected gardens where they could be successfully cultivated. In his report he stated that the North West Company:

(who evince great ability in all their plans and arrangements and avail themselves of every advantage the Country affords) derive great benefit from this source, at Dunvegan, Vermillion, & Fort de Pinnette they have very extensive Gardens which are of the most essential importance to them; last Fall it was particularly exemplified, when the Peace River brigade arrived at Fort Chipewyan, they had no provisions for the remainder of the Voyage, and waited for the arrival of a Canoe load of Potatoes from Vermillion which maintained the people until they arrived at their destinations.[37]

The size and success of gardens further depended on the number of men spending the summer inland as a garden required careful supervision.

Potatoes, turnips, barley, and occasionally peas and onions were usually planted. The men rarely got the gardens in before the first of June, and frost could strike any time after mid-August.[38] This short growing season meant that ideal conditions had to prevail if the fort was to see a harvest. The sandy soil proved a drawback, and a prolonged absence of rain meant almost certain failure. Some prosperous gardens in the mid-1820s led John Franklin to remark "the tables of the officers being supplied daily, and those of the men frequently, with potatoes and barley."[39] During Franklin's visit, a fall planting of barley was made but the results were disappointing.[40] The failure of the gardens in 1832 and 1833 indicates the uncertainties of gardening throughout the early years of Fort Chipewyan.[41]

After a good harvest, there arose the problem of keeping the vegetables from spoiling during the winter. Most of the 1831 harvest, for example, had spoiled by the following May.[42] The meager 1832 crop was exposed to frost, and in an attempt to save some of the potatoes, the men tried freezing them:

> therefore took them out of the cellar, & put them in one of the empty rooms that they may freeze purposefully, for if we leave them to freeze and thaw they will be useless, but by putting them frozen into boiling water & cooking them at once they are still eatable.[43]

The necessity of preserving food reflected the Canadians' capacity to consume it:

> it is well known that all frenchmen are more active in their Employers cause with a full than an Empty Belly - to keep the frenchmen in good humour their chops now and then must be greased.[44]

James Mackenzie described the food in the men's houses:

> In Labris house there are 5 Men, a woman and 3 Children, in La Bicasse's house there are 3 Men and 3 Women, and L'Espagnol's there are two Men and 2 Women - In the first of these Houses they eat about 35 Whitefish every day - in the second 20 do and in the last about 15 do - All these they

devour in three Meals and Sometimes only one - but that is regulated by the Surfeits they take. . . .[45]

James Keith outlined the daily rations for the fort in 1826:

The regular rations of a man on fish is 5 white fish or fresh meat 8-10 [lbs] p diem, conjoined the first part of the winter with 2 lb potatoes on Sundays, afterwards augmented to twice and lastly to thrice that quantity p week, ¼ that allowance for a woman and ¼ for a child. Each dog 2 fish p diem when employed. . . .[46]

Most of the time, the men's diet consisted of a monotonous round of fish-dominated meals.

Often it was either feast or famine. On 4 December 1799, three men ate twenty-three whitefish and a "Dishful of pounded meat & grease."[47] Richardson said in 1833 that boiling the fish was the usual method of cooking them, "so as to form an excellent white soup; but is extremely good when fried, and especially if enveloped in batter."[48] Carp were used to make soup, and eggs of the methy fish made good bread cakes.[49]

Meat—fresh, dried and pounded—was issued when the fisheries failed.[50] In 1824, the men received meat on Sundays, and the wood cutters were given three days' meat rations instead of two every week.[51] Richard King claimed that moose, of all the varieties of fresh meat, was the tastiest because of the softness of the fat. A *dépouille* was the portion of fat, three to six inches thick, which lay next to the skin along the back and rump.[52] These layers of fat were "stripped from the carcass, dipped in hot grease, and hung up in the lodge to dry and smoke before they were ready to be eaten."[53] A *dépouille* served as a substitute for bread.[54] The men valued both the buffalo and the moose for *dépouille*. According to Richard King, however, the best came from a male moose in October.[55] The men considered the nose and tongue of the caribou, moose, and buffalo to be great delicacies.[56]

Flour was scarce, making bannock or *galette* a rare treat.[57] Bannock:

is simply flour and water and grease thoroughly kneaded

and well-baked; the usual method of cooking is to shape the dough an inch deep to the inside of a frying pan, and stand the latter before the camp-fire.[58]

The men also used flour in rubbaboo, which was pemmican boiled in water to make a soup. A touch of sugar improved the mixture's palatability.[59]

The officers fared a little better. Their mess received supplements of butter, sugar, tea, chocolate, pepper, cured ham, Madeira wine, and molasses.[60]

Seasonal produce was all that could relieve the monotony of the men's diet. This could include berries and the eggs of wild birds. In the spring, the women collected the sap from birch trees "for the purpose of making a sirup [sic] used as a substitute for sugar, of which they are extravagantly fond."[61] In 1834, a cow and a calf were shipped by boat from Peace River to Fort Chipewyan "and thereby supplied us with luxuries till then untasted at Chipewyan."[62]

Sadly, starvation was not unknown. During food shortages, the men could be sent to the fisheries to fend for themselves, or out to live with Indian bands.[63] Simpson once reported that the people were "literally starving about the Lake living chiefly on Rock weed; 30 Dollars was given for a dog the other day at the Old Fort which was consumed at one scanty meal."[64] In 1823, Edward Smith reported "several of the Company's dogs missing. Must have been eaten by the men in the spring."[65]

While the fisheries provided for the inhabitants of Fort Chipewyan, the chief concern of the fort in the matter of provisions was to collect an adequate supply of dried provisions for the brigades. To accomplish this, Fort Chipewyan engaged hunters for the winter months.[66] These hunters were either canoe men whose services were not required during the winter, or more often, Cree Indians or Métis. They were equipped with ammunition, tobacco, and food and sent to kill moose, buffalo, and deer in the surrounding country. The hunt for animals centred around

Lake Claire, and ranged as far west as Peace Point on Peace River and north to the Salt Plains west of the Slave River. Apparently five to six days' "march" was considered the limit of the range, but these limits would undoubtedly depend on the size of the kill, the weather, and upon how badly the fort needed provisions. The North West Company, for example, had men hunting buffalo between Portage La Loche and the rapids on Slave River.[67]

Provision accounts taken from surviving journals reveal that an animal rarely yielded more than three hundred pounds of fresh meat for the fort, a fact which suggests the hunters and carters consumed a sizable portion of the meat on the trail. John Charles gave precise details:

> the weight of the moose and buffalo is about 10,051 lbs. nearly 288 lbs. each, the weight of the deer 2283 about 120 each, most of the deer were brought a short distance the consumption therefore considerably less than when fetching the other animals from five and six days March, and the Men of course help themselves liberally on the Journey, as is their usual Custom.[68]

The size of the wood buffalo (*bison bison athabascae* Rhoads) was noted by David Thompson when his party killed two bulls in the vicinity of Ile-à-la-Crosse on 4 June 1812:

> all the Bisons that take to the Woods, become much larger than those of the plains, these were so, their horns from tip to tip measured two feet, and on the curve twenty-eight inches, and when fat [they] must weigh at least two thousand pounds.[69]

J. Dewey Soper corroborates the size of the animals, stating that the average weight for a male is eighteen hundred pounds, and for a female from eight hundred to twelve hundred pounds.[70] Thompson also describes the moose as "the noblest animal of the Forest, and the richest prize the Hunter can take" because of the high value placed on its meat, hide and bones.[71]

There were two methods of hunting by the Indians and these were undoubtedly imitated by the Europeans. Tracking was employed when there were tracks to follow, and tracing was the detection of browsing, rubbing and other signs which an animal left as it travelled.[72] The hunters were likely to have a more successful moose hunt when the snow cover, hardened by frequent thaws and freezes, permitted the use of snowshoes. The moose broke through the crust, thus allowing the hunters to pursue their quarry to an exhausted standstill. The chase might be over in six or eight hours or it could continue for two days.[73]

The moose was more difficult to hunt than the buffalo as it is a wary animal which never permits a hunter to make a direct approach.[74] The buffalo, on the other hand, usually remains unconcerned while a hunter approaches. When aroused, however, the buffalo is much harder to overtake than the short-winded moose.[75] Samuel Hearne gave a vivid account of the wood buffalo chase:

> when pursued they always take to the woods. They are of such an amazing strength, that when they fly through the woods from a pursuer, they frequently brush down trees as thick as a man's arm; and be the snow ever so deep, such is their strength and agility that they are enabled to plunge through it faster than the swiftest Indian can run in snowshoes. . . . I soon found that I was no match for the buffaloes, not withstanding they were plunging through such deep snow, that their bellies made a trench in it as large as if many sacks had been hauled.[76]

After the chase and the killing of a buffalo, the skinning of one of these huge animals was a sizable task:

> they are so heavy, that when six or eight Indians are in company at the skinning of a large bull, they never attempt to turn it over while entire, but when the upper side is skinned, they cut off the leg and shoulder, rip up the belly, take out all the intestines, cut off the head, and make it as light as possible, before they turn it to skin the under side.[77]

After a kill, the hunters sent word to the fort where carters would be immediately dispatched with their sleds and dogs to pick up the meat. The hunters could also cache the meat to be picked up at a later date if the carters were not available.[78] It normally took twelve to thirteen sleds to carry three hundred to four hundred pounds of fresh meat.[79] The average time taken for meat carters to journey to and from Lake Claire was seven days.[80]

Once at the fort, the meat was weighed and stored in the ice house. The one built in 1823 measured twelve feet square and ten feet deep.[81] These houses or cellars held from four thousand to seven thousand pounds of meat, and were covered with ice and snow. Their principal use was to preserve meat in the spring and early summer.

The meat was transported on sledges constructed for that purpose. Daniel Harmon's description is one of the best:

> These sledges are made of two thin boards turned up at the fore end, and joined closely together, so that this vehicle is twelve or fourteen inches broad, and seven or eight feet in length.[82]

Bush sleds differed in construction from the ones used on the lake. The lake sleds did not have the front end boards turned as high as the ones used in the bush where trails often led over low bush and bumpy muskeg.[83] The birch used in making these sleds was collected along the Embarras River after freeze-up.[84]

The dogs that pulled these sleds meant as much to the trapper and trader in winter as their canoes did during the summer. Without dogs to transport the sleds loaded with provisions, the fort could not operate. Peter Fidler and his men were in difficulty in the winter of 1802-03 when, without the assistance of dogs, they had to pull sleds with fish the twenty miles from Old Fort Point. Only the generosity of the XY Company in loaning their dogs and sleds saved the English from a winter of misery.[85] Harmon gives an estimate of the pulling capacity of the dogs:

> Each pair of dogs drew a load of from two hundred, to two hundred and fifty pounds, besides provisions for themselves and their driver, which would make the whole load about

three hundred pounds. I have seen many dogs, two of which would draw on a sledge, five hundred pounds, twenty miles, in five hours.[86]

During the spring and summer the dogs were kept at the fisheries where food was more plentiful.

The first horses to be used at Fort Chipewyan arrived from Peace River in 1804.[87] The men had hoped the horses could haul the sleds loaded with fish to the fort. This proved unsuccessful, however. The shortage of feed and the threat posed to them by the ever-hungry dogs made it difficult to keep them.[88] They were fed fish in 1822.[89] The men's summer duties included the gathering of hay, or more probably swamp grass, for the horses.[90]

The Indians were given ammunition to make fall and spring provision hunts.[91] The fort relied upon the Indians' provision trade for dried or pounded meat and grease to make pemmican. Alexander Mackenzie described the methods of drying meat:

> the lean parts of the flesh of the larger animals are cut in thin slices, and are placed on a wooden grate over a slow fire, or exposed to the sun, and sometimes to the frost.[92]

David Thompson states that dried meat is less than one-third of its former weight[93] and Stefansson says that it is one-sixth of its original weight.[94] He also notes that one pound of dried meat is equal to six pounds of lean meat in food value.[95] Pounded or beat meat was dried meat pounded into shreds and used in making pemmican.

Pemmican making, which was done at the fort, was described by Thomas Simpson:

> The meat, which has been cut into flakes and dried in the sun . . . is conveyed to the establishment. It is there pounded in a mortar, or by beating on an extended hide. The fat is boiled in a cauldron, and skimmed of all impurities; an equal quantity of pounded meat is added to the fat, and the mixture is well stirred and poured hot into skin bags. It hardens in a few hours, and is fit either for immediate use

or to be kept for three to four years.[96]

The fat gave the mixture its palatable qualities. Both Alexander Mackenzie[97] and David Thompson stressed the importance of this ingredient. Thompson described the qualities of buffalo fat:

> the fat of the Bison is of two qualities, called hard and soft; the former is from the inside of the animal, which when melted is called hard fat (properly grease) the latter is made from the hard flakes of fat that lie on each side [of] the backbone, covering the ribs, and which is readily separated, and when carefully melted resembles Butter in softness and sweetness.[98]

Pemmican was held in reserve for longer trips, such as those of the canoe brigades, because it provided the most nutrition in the least bulk. Whereas a man required eight pounds of fish or fresh meat a day, pemmican supplied the equivalent nourishment in one and one-half pounds.[99] R.O. Merriman points out that only fifty-five pounds of pemmican and forty-five pounds of dried meat came from four hundred pounds of fresh meat.[100] The reasons for such a small quantity were the shrinkage caused by drying and the fact that the best pemmican was made from meat that was completely free of gristle and fat.[101] Pemmican, then, was a highly concentrated food that sustained the men of the brigades who had to make contact with the outside world.

Dried meat rather than pemmican was sometimes given to those who travelled shorter distances. On 16 September 1823, James Keith recorded:

> sent 6 men to raise wood for the making of 10 canoes in the spring . . . have provisions for 8 days (140 lbs. dry meat).[102]

Each man was therefore allowed a daily ration of nearly three pounds of dried meat. David Thompson described pemmican bags as thirty inches long, and only four inches thick.[103] Their flat shape suited them to storage in canoes, an important consideration when outfitting a large brigade undertaking a long trip:

> Those brigades which proceed N.W. of Cumberland House
> require three additional bags of pemmican [in addition to
> the two bags for each Saskatchewan canoe] per canoe, and
> some a fourth.[104]

The canoe brigades depended upon pemmican. In 1821,
George Simpson estimated the Athabasca district would
need one hundred bags.[105] To ensure a constant and adequate
supply the traders organized an elaborate provisioning
system.

The fur trade posts on the Peace River supplied much of
the provisions used in the long voyage out in the spring.
The importance of the Peace district to Fort Chipewyan and
the fur trade cannot be overemphasized:

> the Canadians send a single large Canoe up it [Peace River]
> with only three men and fetch down two Tons of dried
> Provisions at a time and this Canoe keeps working most of
> the Summer on purpose to Supply the Athapescow
> Settlement which is the grand Magazine of those parts from
> which the Slave Lake, Peace River and Athapescow River
> Canoes are supplied in the fall of the year and reserve a stock
> of provisions for the Spring. . . .[106]

In August, just before the arrival of the canoes from Lac la
Pluie, a load of provisions would arrive from Peace River
so as to ensure a plentiful supply of food for the brigades.[107]
During the winter, provisions were collected at Fort
Vermilion and Dunvegan; in the spring these were sent to
Fort Chipewyan to supply the outgoing brigades.[108]
Strategically located on the route to the far northwest, Fort
Chipewyan proved to be not only a storehouse for furs but
also for provisions for the district.

During the period of competition, the North West Company
operated a provision post on Lake Claire. Fidler noted the
XY Company had a post on Lake Claire in 1803.[109] These
posts, designed to collect provisions from the Crees, were
apparently abandoned after 1804.[110] In an effort to prevent
the XY Company from trading with the Caribou Eaters, the
North West Company established Fond du Lac at the east

end of Lake Athabasca.[111] This post was closed in 1804 after the Chipewyans killed its men and their wives and children. Pierre au Calumet was established in 1802 for the North West Company near the mouth of Calumet River on the Athabasca River in 1802. It was situated on the east shore, opposite the creek. The post served the Crees and collected provisions for the passing brigades.

Although care was taken to ensure a supply of provisions, there were times when the brigades went hungry. Daniel Harmon met Athabasca brigades who had had nothing to eat for four days.[112] Peter Fidler noted a shortage of provisions in 1804.[113] In 1823 there were only eight bags of pemmican to send with the canoes destined for the forts north and west of Chipewyan.[114] In 1834 Richard King met the brigade:

> At the entrance of Methye Lake we met five boats from Portage La Loche, laden with furs, and containing - men, women, and children - about forty persons, entirely destitute of provisions. They had stripped off the rind of every poplar and birch tree they met with, in order to procure the soft pulpy vessels in contact with the wood; but these, though sweet, are very insufficient to satisfy a craving appetite.[115]

It is impossible to give all the reasons why shortages of provisions occurred without studying the records of the Peace River forts. Some of the reasons at Fort Chipewyan, however, are probably similar to those of the Peace River establishments. The seasons, for example a severe winter or a late fall and spring, were definite factors in provision hunts.[116] The lack of men to gather them was another, especially when the fort was understaffed in summer.[117] When the fisheries failed, the stores of dry meat intended for the brigades had to be used.[118] It is possible that the encouragement of the Indians to hunt small furs, such as muskrat and marten, instead of beaver, caused them to neglect the provision hunts.[119] These smaller animals were easier to kill.

The North West Company had developed the system of supplying provisions, but improvements in the transportation system were made by the Hudson's Bay Company after the 1821 amalgamation. The Northwesters had relied on canoes for transportation because the Canadians, skilled in their construction and operation, were reluctant to use boats. Edward Smith, Chief Factor at Fort Chipewyan in 1822, gave the dimensions of the canoes, known as North canoes:

> Those for the Trade measure about 32 feet from stem to stern, with 4 feet 5 inches, and 2 feet deep at midships, carry 25 pieces, 5 men, not including provisions and mens baggage, thus Equiped they come in 56 days from York Factory to Athabasca Lake last summer. . . .[120]

The area around Fort Chipewyan produced most of the materials required for building canoes. Birch bark was collected toward Birch Mountain along the Birch River.[121] The Canadians used pine instead of cedar because it was plentiful along the Athabasca River. Turnor noted "the Canadians build of the largest size used in the North out of pine."[122] Tar from the oil sands south of Pierre au Calumet mixed with spruce gum was used as waterproofing.[123]

Canoes, however, were not ideally suited for transportation from Fort Chipewyan. First, the gummed seams cracked in cold weather. Fidler said he rubbed the seams with fat, which was preferable to pitch in cold weather, but it rubbed off easily.[124] Secondly, the canoes had to be gummed several times *en route*. These stops delayed the brigades.[125] The lack of canoe materials at Great Slave Lake proved to be a cause of frustration and delay.[126] The use of canoes rather than boats probably contributed to the closure of the Mackenzie River posts in 1814. The frail craft had to be constantly attended to and thus no thought was given to organizing two brigades for the Mackenzie River region so that canoes could be left at Portage La Loche.

When George Simpson was appointed governor of the Northern Department following the 1821 amalgamation of the North West and Hudson's Bay companies, he applied his boundless energy to making his new department more

Sir George Simpson in 1857. His driving personality earned him the nickname "The Little Emperor." (Hudson's Bay Company Archives, Provincial Archives of Manitoba)

efficient. He centred his reforms on transportation, and began replacing canoes with York boats. The boats could carry more cargo than canoes, and were more durable than their lightweight counterparts. A cargo of furs was usually divided into "pieces," each piece being one ninety-pound fur pack (see Appendix). Ten North canoes, carrying approximately 250 pieces, employed fifty to sixty men; four boats, carrying approximately two hundred pieces, employed twenty-five to thirty-two men. Edward Smith reported that the change-over meant an immediate reduction of sixteen men,[127] and fewer men meant fewer provisions. One estimate suggested each outgoing boat required eight bags of pemmican to travel to Cumberland House, while each canoe needed five bags.[128] Furthermore, fewer people would have to be kept at the fort to collect canoe materials.[129]

While Colin Robertson realized the advantages of boats during his Athabasca campaign against the North West Company[130] they were not used at Fort Chipewyan until 1823. The winter of 1822-23 proved to be a busy one for Robert Clouston, the boat-builder. He first had to find wood suitable for keels. The keels of the York boats, constructed of red pine or larch, were shaped without any splicing or joinings.[131] After two weeks of searching, he located some suitable wood.[132] The other problems Clouston encountered included the situation where "oakum, and iron is getting so scarce that [we] have to get gun barrels beat out into nails. . . ."[133] He used linen for caulking.[134] He received proper recognition for his work, completed under difficult conditions, when the boats finally embarked:

> This afternoon Mr. Smith sent off 4 boats for the Portage La Loche with a load of 34 Pks furrs & 1 keg Castn each - 7 men each boat & passengers . . . they left the rock at 2 p.m. - the first boats of the kind that ever sailed on Athabasca Lake - fired 2 shots with our canon on the occasion.[135]

York boats were there to stay.

In his 1823-24 report James Keith compared the financial advantage of boats over canoes for the Athabasca district. Ten canoes and four boats brought in 429 pieces valued at £4,162 10s. 4d.[136] The boats carried 209 pieces worth £2,000 3s. 5d. and the canoes carried 220 pieces valued at £2,162 6s. 11d. If an average of five men per canoe and eight men per boat is assumed, then fifty canoemen brought £2,161 6s. 11d. while thirty-two boatmen brought £2,000 3s. 5d. Clearly, the saving effected by the change from canoes to boats was considerable.[137]

Thus, by the mid-1820s, a reasonably successful system of transportation and provision supply had been developed. Without the constraints of competition, traders no longer had to worry about their provisions being cut off by the actions of rivals. While natural disasters could still interrupt the supply, the system as a whole functioned much more smoothly and dependably. The advent of the York boat streamlined transportation operations and proved to be a saving in manpower as well. With the decline of canoes, however, a particularly colourful and even romantic era of the fur trade was over. The cumbersome York boat could not compete with the elegant style of its more graceful predecessor.

4. THE FORT AND THE MEN WHO SERVED IT

The success of the trade at Fort Chipewyan depended largely on the administrative abilities and personal qualities of the men who conducted its business. The isolation of the fort and its importance as an entrepot for the northern districts meant that sound, experienced leadership was important. Yet the fort could not function without the *engagés*, the labourers upon whose brawny backs the trade depended. The surviving journals reveal that the men who composed the administrative and labouring force of the fort were men willing to seek a new life, perhaps fortune, on the frontiers of civilization. Possibly a life of freedom attracted some; others were lured by the promise of a better income which, if saved over years of service, would lead to purchasing land "back home" where they could live out the remainder of their lives in comparative ease. To gain these goals the men of the northern forest gave up their youth and vigour to the environment; but in return, they lived a free life of a different hue and culture.

While these men were ordinarily engaged to serve in the peaceful pursuit of gathering fur, during the periods of competition between rival traders, life at Fort Chipewyan could often include strife and violence. In the struggle between the companies men were hired for their fighting abilities. Although the life of the fort tended to revolve about seasonal activities, the conflicts between the companies often upset the pattern and character of fort life. The violence reached its peak between 1815 and 1820. Many of the journals and accounts of the trade on Lake Athabasca, written during periods of competition, emphasize the conflicts. The routine activities of the forts are not described, and yet it must be assumed that while some of these activities went on, others were left unattended to give priority to competition.

During these periods the men spent much of their time

watching their opponents' activities. Watchtowers became part of the structure of each fort. Whenever a party set out from one fort, a rival group followed. Often these groups were heading out to live with particular Indian bands and trade directly with them in their camps, a trading method known as *en derouine*. Rivals kept a close watch on one another to prevent the other from getting an advantage. The North West Company, which held its superiority in numbers until the last year or so of the 1815-20 conflict, also sent men to watch the rival brigades moving inland. Their policy, as Peter Fidler noted, was to prevent their rivals carrying on a provisions trade with the Indians along the way.[1]

An engraving of Alexander Mackenzie. (Public Archives of Canada, C-1348)

A.S. Morton stated that the rivalry between the North West Company and the XY Company "habituated the men of both parties to violence."[2] The XY Company, under the leadership of Alexander Mackenzie, sought to wrest the control of the Athabasca trade from the Northwesters between 1798 and 1804, an attempt that ended in failure. The Hudson's Bay Company also attempted to garner some of the Athabasca trade, but in a more peaceful manner. Fidler's journals reveal that the XY Company was very helpful and cooperated with the men from the Bay. This attitude was no doubt motivated by the fact that the more opposition the Northwesters had, the more likely their company was to lose its ascendancy in the trade. While the violence continued between the Canadian companies,[3] the North West Company also kept a close watch on the Hudson's Bay Company and obstructed its trade by not allowing the Indians to barter either furs or provisions with the English.

With the amalgamation of the North West and XY companies in 1804, the new Canadian company turned its combined forces against the inadequately staffed English. Fidler was told that the

> Proprietors of the North West Company were resolutely determined that the servants of the Hudson Bay Company should walk over their bodies than they would allow an Indian to go into the Hudson's Bay Company House. . . .[4]

The men from the Bay were no match for the superior forces of the Canadians. The Hudson's Bay Company required a change in organization, policies and methods if the Northwesters were to be met on an equal footing.

During competition, then, a fort's first duties were to send men *en derouine,* and to keep a close watch on rival traders. Consequently, some of the regular fort duties were probably sacrificed to the demands of competition. After 1821, journals describe the regular routine in greater detail than do the earlier journals.

The Hudson's Bay Company was run from London, England, by the London Committee. The Governor was directly responsible to the Committee; in turn, the Chief Factors, who were each responsible for the operation of a major fur trading post and district, reported to the Governor. The North West Company, on the other hand, was a conglomeration of partners who all shared in the Company's profits. Wintering partners spent the winter at their posts in the interior while the merchant partners remained in Montreal to market the furs and import trade goods.

The men who served these companies in the Athabasca district came from different backgrounds. In both the North West Company and the Hudson's Bay Company the chief officers, the traders and clerks were usually Scottish or English. The North West Company recruited its *engagés* from Lower Canada, whereas the Bay men were recruited from the Orkney Islands. The North West Company also engaged Iroquois for their skill in voyaging and hunting. These varied backgrounds caused differences in the way the trade was carried on. For example, the Canadians and Iroquois, while unsurpassed in the handling of canoes, found it difficult to adjust to the larger, more cumbersome York boats used after 1821.

The *engagés* formed the largest group of men employed in the trade. Men suitable for service in the Athabasca had to be seasoned voyageurs. They were hired for their strength and skill in manning the canoes that carried the goods for the trade. The work that separated a true *homme du nord* from a "pork-eater"[5] was the long voyage over the Churchill system and the Portage La Loche to the Athabasca. An excellent *esprit de corps* apparently existed among the Athabasca voyageurs as they paddled inland. Duncan McGillivray tells of an incident that indicates the pride which these canoemen took in their work:

> The Athabasca Men piqued themselves on a superiority they were supposed to have over the other bands of the north for expeditious marching, and ridiculed our men *à la façon du Nord* for pretending to dispute a point that universally decided in *their* favor. Our people [the Saskatchewan

brigade] were well aware of the disadvantages they laboured under (being heavier loaded than their opponents) but they could not swallow the haughtiness and contempt with which they thought themselves treated, and tho' they could flatter themselves with no hopes of success from the event they resolved to dispute the Victory. . . . In consequence . . . the two Bands instead of camping according to order, entered the Lake at sunset. . . . They pursued the voyage with unremitting efforts without any considerable advantage for 48 hours during which they did not once put ashore, 'till at length, being entirely overcome with labour and fatigue, they mutually agreed to camp. . . .[6]

"Canadian Voyageurs of Capt'n Franklin's Canoe," by Captain Basil Hall. Captain Hall sketched these voyageurs during his travels in North America in 1827 and 1828. (Public Archives of Canada, C-9461)

Each North canoe carried a crew of between five and eight men. A full complement of eight men consisted of a bowman, a steersman, and six middlemen. The bowman, sitting in the bow, acted as the guide for the canoe. The six middlemen sat in pairs, about five feet apart, in the middle of the canoe. The steersman sat, or stood, in the stern of the canoe.[7] A guide responsible for the safety of the canoes and their contents conducted each brigade. These guides were noted for the speed and efficiency at which their brigades travelled.

The cargo for each canoe greatly concerned the canoemen. George Back gives a description of how the pieces were allocated for the North canoes at Fort William:

> The Canadian *voyageur* is, in all respects, a peculiar character; and on no point is he . . . more *touchy* than in the just distribution of "pieces" among the several canoes forming a party. . . . The usual mode is for the guide to distribute or portion them out by lots, holding in his hand little sticks of different lengths which the leading men will draw. From the decision so made there is no appeal, and the parties go away laughing or grumbling at their fortunes.[8]

The distribution of the freight affected the speed of the canoes and the length of time spent on portages.

On the voyage, the canoemen were held to a strict daily routine. Rising at the first sign of dawn, they would raise camp and travel three or four hours before stopping for breakfast, the main meal of the day. After breakfast, the brigade would travel until late afternoon or early evening when the men would camp for the night. Lunch was usually a half-hour meal taken without stopping. Each day's travel was divided into what the voyageurs called "pipes." A pipe was the time taken to smoke a pipe along the way, or a distance estimated by the voyageurs to be three leagues. David Thompson, however, found a pipe closer to a distance of two leagues.[9]

The wind was an important factor in voyaging. If it was too boisterous, it held the frail canoes and their cargo windbound. If the breeze blew in their favour, the voyageurs were spared some toil by hoisting a sail. The men had their ways of invoking a favourable breeze:

> Our Iroquois, being tired with the day's journey, and longing for a fair wind to ease their arms, frequently in the course of the afternoon, scattered a little water from the blades of their paddles as an offering to *La Vieille*, who presides over

the wind. The Canadian voyageurs, ever ready to adopt the Indian superstitions, often resort to the same practice, though it is probable that they give only partial credence to it.[10]

One solution to the wind problem meant rising at two or three o'clock in the morning before the wind came up on the wide rivers and lakes, and beginning the day's travel then.

George Back made an interesting comparison between the handling of boats and canoes in 1833:

> the River Maligne [north of Cumberland House] . . . may with perfect propriety be described as one uninterrupted rapid; and was at that period so low, that the boats had to treble their distance in going backwards and forwards for the cargo. A glance at their manner of working was enough to satisfy me of their capability. . . . Still the contrast between us was great [Back was in a canoe with 8 men]; and my skilful guide De Charloit (a half-breed), did not fail to make the superiority of the canoe appear to the best advantage. The cumbrous *bateaux* were dragged laboriously, a few paces at a time, by the united exertions of those on board and those on shore. Sometimes, unable to resist the impetuous force of the current, they were swept back; at others, suspended on the arched back of a descending wave, they struggled and laboured until they were again in the shelter of a friendly eddy. But the canoe, frail as she was, and too weak for the encounter of such rude shocks, was nevertheless threaded through the boiling rapids and sunken rocks with fearful elegance. The cool dexterity with which she was managed was truly admirable; not a "set" was missed. . . .[11]

Back describes a "set" as "the firm fixing of the pole against the bottom of the river, and a false set has often occasioned the loss of a canoe."[12]

Portaging was the most onerous task. The Portage La Loche, which separates the waters of the Mackenzie basin from those of the Hudson Bay, was the portage that presented the greater trial of strength. One of the few accounts of crossing the portage is given by John Richardson. He states that the average load of the Canadian on a longer portage was two pieces, each weighing ninety pounds, "and in shorter ones, often a greater load."[13] Each man received an equal number of packs, in addition to carrying the boats and their equipment. The ordinary or expected carry was two miles a day which, if each man carried five pieces, meant walking approximately twenty miles, ten of these with a load.[14] There were nine resting places along the portage.

This rather romantic engraving by Sir George Back is entitled the "Vale of the Clearwater River from the Methye Portage, 1828." At the north end of the portage, the land drops 210 metres to the Clearwater River below. (Public Archives of Canada, C-94110)

Numerous discomforts added to the miserable work of portaging. One explorer noted:

> For about six or seven miles on this portage, the voyageurs are exposed to temporary but acute suffering, from the total absence of good water to quench the thirst, aggravated, in our case, by carrying loads of 200 lbs, in an atmosphere of 68° Fahrenheit.[15]

Horse-flies or "bull-dogs," and mosquitoes also added to the misery of portaging.[16]

Effectual leadership made a successful journey possible. John Richardson noted:

> with so short a travelling season, every hour is of importance, and whoever has charge of a party must show that he thinks so, otherwise his men cannot be induced to keep up their exertions for sixteen hours a day, which is the usual period of labour in summer travelling.[17]

Captain Back is again the artist of this watercolour idealizing the view from the Methy Portage. The portage crossed the height of land that separates the Hudson Bay and Arctic Ocean's drainage basins, and the expansive view at its west end impressed all who saw it. (Public Archives of Canada, C-2477, 73-1-33)

Richardson implies that without energetic leadership, the common men often lacked the willingness or readiness to carry out their duties properly. In 1791, for example, Philip Turnor reported that the North West Company men left their canoes and returned to the fort, having been forced by ice conditions to give up their journey. Roderick Mackenzie thereupon went back out with the men and hauled the canoe over the ice to the Slave River which was still open.[18]

The voyageurs took pride in their appearance upon arrival at the fort:

Sept. 19, 1820 - Landed at 6 PM in order to give our men time to wash their things as they are desirous to appear in good feather on their arrival at the fort.[19]

It was only the following day at the entrance to the lake that the men changed into clean clothes.[20] George Back, while voyaging inland to Chipewyan in 1833, gives a brief description of the finery and some unhappy results:

The crew had dressed themselves out in all their finery, - silver bands, tassels, and feathers in their hats, - intending to approach the station with some effect, but, unhappily for the poor fellows, the rain fell in torrents, their feathers drooped. . . .[21]

When the brigade arrived at the fort, the officers, who had arrived earlier in light canoe, immediately set to work unpacking, checking and repacking the pieces for distribution to posts on the Peace and Mackenzie rivers.[22] The outfits, as the year's supplies were called, were dispatched to the most distant posts first. The New Caledonia canoes left in early September, followed by the Mackenzie River, Peace River, and Great Slave Lake brigades.[23] Many of the voyageurs manned the canoes destined for the far districts. The rest of the men began to prepare for the long freeze that was winter at Fort Chipewyan.

The advent of the York boat after 1821 meant the colourful brigades were gradually phased out. The boats had to be pulled over portages, too heavy to be carried like the lighter canoes. At the arduous Methy Portage, goods were unloaded from the boats left at each end of the Portage, it being too long to haul the boats across. The brigade that had travelled from Red River to the east end of the Portage exchanged its provisions and supplies for the furs from the northern districts brought by the brigades from Fort Chipewyan to the western end of the Portage.

With the work hard and the living conditions Spartan, the fur trade drew independent, irascible men to its labouring ranks. They were men who had left civilization far behind, and their pride and temper swelled to fill the gap that separated them from it. Richardson recounted the case of an old voyageur who bet his entire salary that his dogs, "poor and lean as they were," would travel to Fort Chipewyan in less time than the others. His confident manner came from the fact

> that the voyagers of the Athabasca department consider themselves as very superior to any other. The only reasons he could assign were: that they had borne their burdens across the terrible Methye Portage, and that they were accustomed to live harder and more precariously.[24]

Back related how one Canadian was embarrassed by frost-bite, "for there is a pride amongst 'Old Voyagers' which makes them consider the state of being frost-bitten as effeminate, and only excusable in a 'Pork-eater' or one newly come into the country."[25] John Franklin had to threaten his men with severe punishment to maintain control over them:

> having learned from the gentlemen, most intimately acquainted with the character of the Canadian voyagers, that they invariably try how far they can impose upon every new master with whom they may serve, and that they will continue to be disobedient and intractable if they once gain any ascendency over him.[26]

Their independent character, developed through situations where survival had often been their only objective, did not readily lend itself to discipline.

Mackenzie also spoke of the improvidence of the Canadians who, in his viewpoint, rivalled "the savages in a neglect of the morrow."[27] The physical and mental toughness made the Canadian men, in spite of their faults, a class of workers able to endure the hardships of fort life. Orkneymen were regarded, however, as superior fishermen because they took better care of their nets and the fish that they caught.[28] Although James Keith thought that Orkneymen would make better boatmen than the Canadians, he concluded that they were not suited to long summer voyages and the irregular routine of winter. "Jean Baptiste therefore with all his peculiarities, capricious leanings . . . must constitute our principal Physical prop," Keith concluded.[29]

Although the hours of work were long, there was time for some leisure activity. During the North West Company period, Fort Chipewyan was noted for its library. Roderick Mackenzie had begun the library, but in 1814 Ferdinand Wentzell reported that "scarcely a complete set of books can be found."[30] Nevertheless, thirty-six years later, Henry Lefroy found "many sound books of history and general literature."[31] Colin Robertson read five volumes of Shakespeare's works during his imprisonment in Fort Chipewyan in 1818-19.[32]

The officers often took up hunting for a pastime, especially in the spring and fall when geese and ducks were plentiful.[33] Lefroy noted that during the winter, "a sort of dreamy inactivity takes the place of other enjoyments."[34] He described his daily routine:

> We breakfast at 9, tea and moose steaks, after breakfast I go to the observy. . . . Sometimes I join them at dinner, which invariably consists of whitefish *au naturel*, i.e., without bread, sauce or vegetable. Supper the same as breakfast, except that at the latter we enjoy the additional luxury of potatoes, not at the other. After tea I play chess for a couple of hours. . . .[35]

The arrival of a visitor brought an air of festivity to the fort:

> Flag staff shaped with new flag and the same was saluted with a few shots from a small cannon. We intended this ceremony for the arrival of our friends from below. They disappointed us by arriving at night.[36]

Dances also provided entertainment in the off hours.[37] Certain holidays were customarily observed: 1 November, All Saints Day, was set aside for the men; and, of course, Christmas and New Year's festivities were never missed. During the times liquor was allowed, the celebrations often continued for a week or more.[38] New Year's Day usually commenced with the firing of guns, followed by a treat of brandy and cakes.[39] John Charles estimated the expenses for New Year's, 1832:

> 81 lbs Grease 56 lbs D Meat 257 Fresh Meat 29 quarts barley 50 B Meat [beat or pounded meat] 4½ Kegs Potatoes & each of these Men got a Pipe & 2 feet tobacco.[40]

Charles had, according to his custom, smuggled in some rum, which undoubtedly added to the merriment.

The custom of fur traders marrying Indian women "à la façon du nord" not only provided men isolated from the comforts of European civilization with the companionship of mates and the comforts of family life, but also gave the rest of the fort an excuse for a celebration. George Simpson gave an entertaining account of the events which led up to the "treat":

> Mr. Greill alleges that the object of his present visit is to receive a supply of goods, I am not however inclined to give him credit for all the merit he claims, in having performed a four days journey in two and a half alone, and at this season of the year, out of pure zeal in the cause of his employers, and he at length admits that Cupid in some measure prompted him in the undertaking; the fact is, that he came to reclaim a frail fair one, who during his absence at the Depot, put herself under the protection of Mr. Brown; each Gentleman advanced powerful claims to the Prize, it was at length agreed through my suggestion, that the Lady should be permitted to take her choice, and after some consideration she cast a sheeps towards the Vetran, who in the evening gave a treat to the people as customary on such felicitous events.[41]

Such marriages also allowed the traders to establish permanent contact with the Indians. When the Hudson's Bay Company began to discourage such unions, George Simpson disagreed:

> the restrictions which the Honble Committee have put on Matrimonial alliances and which I consider most baneful to the interests of the Company are tantamount to a prohibition

of forming a most important chain of connection with the Natives. . . .[42]

The alternative, Simpson pointed out, was a greater dependence upon the Indians who, he maintained,

> have no other feelings than those which interest and mercenary views create towards us; it is never matured to attachment and a price is only required to make those *on whom our existance* depends our inveterate Enemies.[43]

Mackenzie had noted that a Chipewyan father had the right of "disposing of his daughter."[44] He added, however, that they did not "sell them as slaves, but as companions *to those who are supposed to live more comfortably than themselves*."[45] Not all traders, however, treated Indian women with consideration. Mackenzie related the story of an Indian woman who had left her husband:

> This Indian brought his daughter, who deserted in the course of the winter from Morin, at Slave Lake, in order to be returned to her husband (Morin). Mr. Porter wrote me, by Morin's orders to sell her to the highest bidder and debit Morin for the amount. . . . I therefore kept the woman to be disposed of when the Peace River Bucks begin to rutt most, I mean in the month of May.[46]

The abuse of Indian women at the hands of fur traders caused friction between the Indians and the whites. The Chipewyans asked Mackenzie to stop the "traffic" in women, as he phrased it.[47] He replied, "[W]e would do as we thought proper."[48]

Sometimes, however, the fur trader was encouraged in his abuse of Indian women by Chipewyan behaviour. The Chipewyans made a practice of wrestling for women: the woman had no choice but to go to the victor. Samuel Hearne described one such wrestling match:

> the whole business consists of hauling each other about by the hair of the head: they are seldom known either to strike or kick one another. It is not uncommon for one of them to cut off his hair and to grease his ears, immediately before

the contest begins. This, however, is done privately; and it is sometimes truly laughable, to see one of the parties strutting about with an air of great importance, and calling out, "Where is he? Why does he not come out?" when the other will bolt out with a clean shorned head and greased ears, rush on his antagonist, seize him by the hair, and though perhaps a much weaker man, soon drag him to the ground. . . .[49]

Hearne also tells of his party coming across a woman who had lost her way. Before the evening was over, "the poor girl was actually won and lost at wrestling by near half a score of different men."[50] The fur traders participated in this practice and, interpreting it as evidence of the Chipewyan male's contemptuous treatment of women, often treated Chipewyan women with similar disdain.

John Charles could not help remarking with some disdain on other activities initiated by the women:

> some of the women in the summer furnish ammunition to these fellows to kill Ducks for them, and at the same time take occasional excursions with them in their canoes; *the rest* may be guessed at.[51]

In an effort to improve standards of conduct, an attempt was made to keep Sunday as the Sabbath:

> That for the more effectual civilization and moral improvement of the families attached to the different establishments and the Indians—Every Sunday when circumstances permit, divine Service be publicly read with becoming solemnity, either once or twice a day, to be regulated by the number of people and other circumstances, at which every man woman and child resident must attend, together with such of the Indians who may be at hand, as it may be found proper to admit.[52]

This regulation, and several others of a similar nature, were duly read and posted. Those who did not comply with the new regulations had their rations withdrawn for one day.[53]

The *engagés'* labour powered the vast machine that was the

nineteenth-century fur trade. Whether paddling the canoes or manning the fort fishery, each man's role was critical to the machine's efficient operation. A successful trade, however, did not depend only on the men who served at Fort Chipewyan and in the larger fur trade organization. The trade also needed the cooperation of the Indians who hunted the furs and were willing to trade them for European goods.

5. THE INDIANS, FORT CHIPEWYAN, AND THE METHODS OF TRADE

As was the case at most forts throughout the Northwest, the traders at Fort Chipewyan soon learned the Indians were the decisive factors in a successful trade. The traders discovered they had to develop trading methods that acknowledged Chipewyan cultural traits. Samuel Hearne's account of the Northern Indians provides a glimpse of a society largely unaffected by European culture.[1] The traders had to take this into account and devise trade practices that exploited the Indians' way of living.

This chapter discusses some aspects of the Chipewyans' cultural and physical environment as they came into contact with the fur trade and the European civilization of which it was a part, and attempts to delineate how the fur traders tried to turn these factors to their advantage. The traders were further constrained by conditions of monopoly or competition as well as by natural disasters such as epidemics. Through the traders' eyes, however, the Indians, Fort Chipewyan and the methods of trade existed solely to serve the needs of the fur trading company.

Alexander Mackenzie described the geographical position of the Chipewyans as lying between latitudes 60° and 65° north, and longitudes 100° and 110° west.[2] Samuel Hearne said their boundaries extended from 59° to 68° north latitude, and from the west coast of Hudson Bay westward for five hundred miles. The Churchill River formed the southern boundary.[3] J. Richardson gave this country the unflattering label "the barren lands."

According to Diamond Jenness, the Chipewyans' original or pre-1689 lands were around Churchill. He attributes their dispersion to the coming of the fur trade.[4] A.S. Morton claims that the Crees drove the Chipewyans to the barren grounds in the eighteenth century.[5] The development of the Indian middleman trading organization was probably also a cause.[6] The extent of their lands, however, gave the Chipewyans an advantage over other tribes:

> they can never be rendered dependant, much less become stationary . . . as many of the other Indian tribes, from the obvious circumstance of having their lands to resort to when caprice or necessity prompt them retiring thither.[7]

The Chipewyan followed the enormous caribou herds in their seasonal journeys across the barrens.[8] This permitted them, if they wished, to act independently of the European trader. Hearne claimed that the Indian method of hunting animals by capturing them in pounds was so successful that it caused

> a habitual indolence in the young and active, who frequently spend a whole Winter in this indolent manner: and as those parts of the country are almost destitute of every animal of the fur kind, it cannot be supposed that those who indulge themselves in this indolent method of procuring food can be masters of anything for trade. . . .[9]

Hearne was the first to characterize Chipewyan behaviour in terms of fur trade participation. One group, the fur traders, he labelled "the more industrious" because they travelled to Churchill to exchange furs for trade goods. After the establishment of Fort Chipewyan these Indians moved to the country between Great Slave and Athabasca lakes because it harboured many fur-bearing animals. The fort also made trade goods more easily available. No longer did the Indians need to undertake the arduous trip to Hudson Bay:

> one half of the inhabitants, and perhaps the other half also, are frequently in danger of being starved to death . . . most of these scenes of distress happen during their journies to and from Prince of Wales's Fort. . . .[10]

The journey of five to six months was only undertaken when "necessity obliges them."[11]

Philip Turnor also mentioned that the Indians

> all agree that they are well used at Churchill and get plenty
> for their furrs but that the distance is so very great that it
> fatigues them very much occasions great loss of time that
> they live very hard upon the journey and frequently many
> of them starve to death particularly if they go in winter and
> if they go in Summer they have a great number of rivers to
> pass near the factory the crossing of which puts them to great
> inconvenience and they do not know the way by the rivers
> as untill within this few years the Indians that inhabit the
> low countries was at war with them which obliged them to
> take a more Northern rout and instead of navigating the
> rivers only to cross them. . . .[12]

A winter journey thus involved a distinct possibility of
starvation, because the chief source of food, the caribou,
moved south and west from the barren grounds into forest
protection at the onset of cold weather.

Travel during the summer was equally difficult because the
Chipewyans only used canoes to ford streams and rivers.[13]
Nor were these canoes suitable for navigation of any distance
because, although they were large enough for two people,

> one . . . lies down at full length for fear of making the canoe
> top-heavy, and the other sits on his heels and paddles.[14]

George Simpson also characterized Indian behaviour using
a fur trader's standard:

> they shook off their indolent habits, became expert Beaver
> hunters, and now penetrate in search of that valuable animal
> into the Cree and Beaver hunting Grounds, making a circuit
> easterly by Carribeau Lake; to the South by Isle a la Crosse;
> and Westerly to the Bank of Peace River. . . . The greater
> portion of them however remain on their own barren lands,
> where they procure sustenance with little exertion as the
> Country abounds with Rein Deer, and some years nearly the
> whole of them resort thither, at times influenced by
> superstitious feelings, and others by having laid up what
> they consider an abundant Stock of European articles (being
> very provident) in order to indulge in ease and luxury. . . .[15]

The traders felt that those who remained on their lands had a much easier life than those who took up trapping. Hearne, not understanding Chipewyan culture, noted with disgust that "ambition never leads them to anything beyond the means of procuring food and clothing."[16]

This second group became known as "caribou eaters."[17] Since they tended to remain on their lands, they were of less economic value to the fur trade. The traders at Fort Chipewyan tried to encourage more of the Caribou Eaters to take up trapping and thus frequent the trading post. Peter Fidler identified their problem in 1804:

> few Indians are about & what has been in have all gone directly for their lands to the Eastward & will not be in before next November and then will have little or nothing in with them as all that country is destitute of Beaver - abounding only in Deer, the Skins of which they require to make their Winter rigging of. . . .[18]

In 1825, James Keith, although anxious to reduce the number of Indians about the fort, did not want to see them return to their lands: "Others talk of going to their lands, at which I Pretend the most perfect indifference, conceiving it the most effectual mode of preventing them."[19] Some of them did, however, and as a result the returns fell in 1826.[20]

The fur traders also tried to exploit what they saw as a weakness in the Chipewyans' character, their timid, peaceable nature, when faced with a stronger opponent. When faced with a weaker opponent, however, the Chipewyans often took the offensive. Samuel Hearne commented that "they take every advantage of bodily strength to rob their neighbours."[21] The fur traders observed this behaviour, and used it to their advantage. The North West Company found it was easier to get furs from the Chipewyans by demonstrating a show of force or numbers.[22] When there was competition for furs, the North West Company simply forced the Chipewyans to trade with them by employing superior numbers.

The practice of sending men *en derouine* not only encouraged them to make good hunts, but also ensured they would bring their furs to the right company.[23] An entry in the Nottingham House Journals for 1802, a Hudson's Bay Company post, read:

> Several Chipewyans went away, the Old Company [North West Company] are sending men with them to prevent the Indians from giving us any Skins - had we men here to spare, we could have sent away some also . . . but the want of hands prevents me, & must trust to the Honesty of the Indians altogether; which in general is pretty good had they the liberty of giving their skins where they chose - but they are very much intimidated by the Old Coy & if they are known to give a skin elsewhere, they are sure to receive a good drubbing. . . .[24]

Numerical superiority was an important factor when companies competed for furs because it seemed to impress the Chipewyans. For example, when John Clarke arrived in the Athabasca district, he made an impressive show of force by keeping light canoes of men "continually running about."[25] On another occasion,

> Their vaunting Commander in Chief with a number of his field officers and *Flag* came over in two light canoes, crowded with men, making a pompous Display of a multiplicity of warlike impliments.[26]

The Chipewyans would not antagonize a force they considered superior to their own, as Alexander Mackenzie noted:

> They make war on the Esquimaux, who cannot resist their superior numbers, and put them to death, as it is a principal with them never to make prisoners. At the same time they tamely submit to the Knisteneaux [Crees] who are so numerous as themselves, when they treat them as enemies.[27]

In the final conflict between the Northwesters and the Hudson's Bay men, a major reason for the defection of the Chipewyans from the North West Company was their realization that the English were just as powerful as the Canadians.

From the Indians' viewpoint, another important factor influencing the choice of trading partners was the quantity and quality of trade goods. The traders were surprised by the Chipewyans' bargaining expertise, and soon realized trading would not be the simple exchange they had hoped. Alexander Mackenzie quickly labelled this forthright behaviour fraudulent and deceitful,[28] when in effect the Chipewyans were simply trying to ensure their own interests were not overlooked.

The fur traders were also deeply puzzled by the Indians' indifference to accumulating large quantities of material goods. Samuel Hearne called them "the greatest philosophers, as they never give themselves the trouble to acquire what they can do well enough without."[29] The fur traders realized slowly, if at all, that Chipewyan concepts of property and commercial value did not correspond to European ones.[30] Certainly by the middle of the eighteenth century many Indians had come to depend on certain European goods, such as hunting or cooking utensils, and traded to obtain these articles. Once these articles had been obtained, however, they preferred to trade for items they could use or consume immediately rather than acquire vast quantities of material goods that would only encumber their nomadic lifestyle.

The traders soon learned the Chipewyans would not trap unlimited numbers of furs because they had little interest in trading for articles they did not need or could not use immediately. To maximize their profits, then, the fur traders had to devise methods of persuading the Indians to hunt more and more furs. This became most important during periods of competition when a choice of trading partners gave the Chipewyans the upper hand in choosing options and driving bargains. Therefore, both the North West Company and the Hudson's Bay Company sought to monopolize a trading district to ensure a successful return of furs. Under competition, the traders realized that simply offering the Indians higher prices for their furs would not solve their problem: the Indians would require even fewer furs to obtain the items they wanted.[31] Not to be thwarted, however, the fur traders sought other ways to earn good returns when the European system of price and supply failed them. These methods came from the traders' adjustment to Chipewyan culture.

Indian trade habits involved an exchange of pleasantries and generalities before the bargaining began. This social aspect, as the traders labelled it, was the key to a successful trade. The Indians based their bargaining on the idea of an exchange of gifts. These gratuities were, under monopoly, a "bit of tobacco and a dram."[32] During competition the minimum gift increased in quantity because the Indians could bargain at more than one post. The trader who offered many gratuities would have the opportunity for a more successful trade because the Indians would at least be present in his trading hall.

In an effort to entice the Indians to hunt and trade furs consistently, the traders placed a great emphasis on making chiefs of some of the more productive hunters. The Chipewyans tended to roam about in small groups in search of food, clothing and shelter. The leaders of these groups acted more like guides than chiefs as no real need for the latter existed. The Indians did, however, realize the importance of a leader when they went to trade their furs:

> it is an universal practice with the Indian Leaders, both Northern and Southern, when going to the Company's Factory, to use their influence and interest in canvassing for companions; as they find by experience that a large gang gains them much respect . . . the authority of those great men, when absent from the Company's Factory, never extends beyond their own family. . . .[33]

The traders named the chiefs to promote the trade. James Keith observed in 1825 that

> their influence & authority being little known beyond the circle of their own Family & immediate dependents. . . . Their estimation & treatment by Whites which are dependant on and regulated by their general habits & exertions, never

fail to insure the Individual a proportionate share of attention or contempt from his own tribe - Like the coin of a Kingdom, they require the stamp & impression of the Sovereign to indicate their value & rend them Current.[34]

Richardson also noted the custom in the late 1840s, stating, "At present, the rank of a chief is not fully established among his own people until it is recognized at the fort to which he resorts."[35] These chiefs became influential in Indian society only in bartering furs.

Once recognized as a chief, an Indian was entitled to a place of first importance at the fort. Upon approaching the fort, he would send a messenger ahead to announce his impending arrival.[36] The trader would then, if the chief's past performance warranted it, send tobacco and liquor to him.[37] His arrival at the fort was often greeted with a "salute of Fire arms and hoisted flags."[38] He and his band then were treated with more tobacco and liquor.

The next important step involved the clothing of a chief. James Mackenzie described the ceremony, an occasion on which he distributed tobacco and part of a keg of mixed rum to five chiefs, thereby saving some expense to his employers:

> they seemed quite happy with their good luck. Had these presents been given to these "great men" separately, it would not have appeared half so much, nor have been enough to content them.
>
> Several harangues suitable to the occasion were made on both sides. . . . He made many ceremonies before he accepted of the laced coat; he wished to have a red great coat, short breeches and cotton stockings, like the English Chief some years ago at the Old Fort. . . . In short his head was already so intoxicated by his change of fortune, that he did not know which end of him stood uppermost, whether he . . . walked or flew. . . .[39]

The custom was carried out in a similar manner by the Hudson's Bay Company in 1823 when four chiefs were outfitted.[40] At this time each chief received a keg of liquor, a suit of clothing, and four feet of tobacco. After the Company discontinued the use of liquor, the chiefs still continued to receive their outfits of clothing.[41]

The fall visit was the most important one for the Indians because the fort's trade goods had arrived from the east. After the arrival of the brigades, the officers gave the Indians their debts for the ensuing season. The system of giving debts simply meant the fort followed the usual custom of the fur trade by giving the Indians their goods on credit in the fall. The Indians departed for their winter hunting grounds after receiving their advances. In the spring, the Indians would presumably pay their debts with their winter's fur catch.

In the opinion of James Keith, the gathering of the Indians at the fort in the fall and their subsequent lengthy visit contributed to the spread of sickness and disease and to a mood of depression among them:

> languor and inaction at one of the most inclement and unwholesome seasons of the year, is . . . productive of a variety of complaints . . . particularly the Chipewyans, others are not so much damped and depressed by their own Complaints, the sickness or mortality of their comrades and relatives, that not only the Fall hunt, but that of half the winter is lost before they recruit their spirits and resume their winter habits of activity and exertion. . . .[42]

Disease caused great hardships among the Indians. Alexander Mackenzie mentioned that "rheumatic pain, the flux and consumption" as well as venereal disease were common.[43] The diseases that caused the greatest trouble were those introduced by the white men and against which the Indians had little immunity. During the summer of 1803, a peculiar illness, which Fidler said was a "stomach complaint with Great lassitude & shortness of breathing,"[44] caused the death of at least thirty-six hunters.[45] This sickness caused the Indians to leave the area around the fort in an effort to escape it.[46] The few Indians who remained accomplished very little owing to the number of deaths.

In 1819-20, William Todd wrote:

> one of the women belonging to the Fort [Wedderburn] has
> taken the Measles the disease appears to have been brought
> in by the families belonging to the NWC. The hooping cough
> has likewise made its appearance, a disease particularly
> distressing among the Indians as its depriving them of the
> means of subsistence, the whole of their caution in
> approaching an animal being rendered abortive by a single
> cough.[47]

Starvation thus faced those families whose hunters were too
ill to hunt.[48] By December, the measles had spread
throughout the district.[49] The Indians naturally had a great
fear of these diseases; in 1833, John Charles told of their
apprehension:

> The fellows have wind of the prevalence of cholera . . .
> having swept off such numbers in Montreal last
> summer. . . . And after having paid them for every thing
> . . . begged to be indulged with large advances to go to their
> lands and not return till next April, to be out of the way of
> sickness. . . .[50]

Infectious diseases could devastate a band and totally disrupt
hunting. Most upsetting to a season's hunt was a death in
a family or band. After a death the Chipewyans observed
a period of mourning that Hearne said could last a year.[51]
Chipewyan custom also required that the Indians destroy
or discard most of their possessions. This custom had a direct
effect upon the fur trade. In 1800, John Porter noted that the
death of one of the hunters had caused the rest to throw
away most of their provisions.[52] And in 1820, William Todd
recorded the result of the measles epidemic:

> the present moment is particularly discouraging for traders,
> the Indians hunted little, yet several of them are almost
> naked having buried the greater part of their clothing with
> their deceased relatives and are now making a demand for
> another supply.[53]

A similar situation was noted in 1833.[54] Fidler, commenting
on the death of three hunters, noted that not only would

their hunting skills be lost, but the deaths had cast "a melancholy gloom on nearly all the rest."[55]

Not only illness and death but also the Indians' spiritual beliefs affected the hunt. Sometimes if they encountered little success in the early part of the season they blamed it on an evil spirit that haunted them. As George Simpson said in 1820,

> they become so full impressed with the idea that some evil genius haunts them, that they give themselves up entirely to despair, they become careless, neglect their hunts, lay dormant in their encampments for weeks together, while a morsel of leather or Babiche remains to keep them in existence. . . .[56]

The situation was no better in 1833,

> The Indians tenting near the House are rather alarmed, they have it that there is *Innab Honnee* as they call them, haunting their movements, that is Bad People who are always in search of mischief but can never be seen . . . and to give it credit they give out that a Chipewyan who left this last Sunday week is missing. . . .[57]

The result was that some of the Indians did not travel to the barren grounds that spring.

Peter Fidler noted aspects of the Indians' belief system in his travels with them during the winter of 1791-92, and how the traders turned aspects of it to their own advantage. Some Canadians had cached ten pieces of trade goods in a log house near the Slave River rapids by what is now Fort Smith. They had "an Image set upon a painted red pole over the house about the size of a small child."[58] Fidler claimed that although the Indians passed by it all winter, not one would venture near the cabin. They were, he maintained,

> thoroughly persuaded that . . . the Een Coz zy as they called it would acquaint the Canadians of the offender which beliefs I further confirmed. . . .[59]

While the fur traders may have had difficulty coming to grips with the Chipewyan belief system, they had no difficulty, as this example illustrates, in using it when it suited their purpose.

The fur traders also sought much more tangible solutions to their fur trading problems. One solution they tried was the use of liquor. By offering the Indians liquor before trading took place, the traders hoped to gain the upper hand in negotiations. To the traders' chagrin, the Chipewyans could not be fooled. Mackenzie noted they usually came to the trading hall with "a regular and uninterrupted use of their understanding, which is always directed to the advancement of their own interest."[60] According to Philip Turnor, when the Chipewyans brought their provisions in to trade in the spring, "The Chipewyan tribe will not trade Liquor consistently, are not fond of parting with their provision, but powder and shot will draw it from them."[61] The Chipewyans were much more interested in trading for ammunition than for liquor.

The Chipewyans were unlike their southern neighbours, the Crees, however, whose taste for liquor was so pronounced that a separate post, Pierre au Calumet, was maintained for them on the Athabasca River. Although provisions were collected at this post, another reason was

> to keep the Northern Indians apart otherwise when they are drinking the Southern Indians are sure to insult the Northern Indians though they should be much inferior in numbers through a supposed superiority in rank. . . .[62]

By maintaining separate posts for the Crees and the Chipewyans, the traders hoped to avoid clashes between the two groups.

As a result of the Chipewyan indifference toward liquor, the Hudson's Bay Company withdrew it from the trade at Fort Chipewyan in 1826. Although the Indians were upset at the regulation and threatened to withdraw to their own lands,[63] the reports and journals after this date show that the rule had little effect upon the returns of the post. John Richardson reported in 1851 that "the present race of Chipewyans are ignorant of the use of spiritous liquors."

The Chipewyans adjusted their trading habits to suit whatever condition, monopoly or competition, existed at the time. Under competition, they quickly seized the advantage it gave them, much to the traders' frustration. James Mackenzie complained that "These damned Rascals delight in nothing more than in Changing forts and in getting Goods for nothing at every place they go."[64] John Porter said that the Indians at Great Slave Lake were demanding "Goods to be Sold here on the Same Conditions as at Fort Chipiwian."[65] After Porter assured them the prices were the same, the Indians "then Said we Should reduce their Last Spring Credits in the Same manner."[66] Porter managed to talk them out of this last demand.

The traders were equally quick to condemn the Chipewyans' behaviour, refusing to understand the Chipewyans were merely acting in their own interest:

> they possess a considerable degree of deceit, and are very complete adepts in the art of flattery, which they never spare as long as they find that it conduces to their interest . . . if the least respect be shown them, it makes them intolerably insolent . . . by giving him [the Indian] the least indulgence . . . he will grow indolent, inactive, and troublesome, and only contrive methods to tax the generosity of an European.[67]

Not only did competition give the Chipewyans the advantage in the bargaining process, it meant they could obtain the goods they wanted for fewer furs. Fidler said one Indian received a complete outfit for his family although "what the man may kill this winter will not pay for ¼ of those articles."[68] Prior to the union of the Canadian companies in 1804, he reported the

> Inds. killing very few furrs. Indeed they have very little occasion to work as they are liberally supplied betwixt those two Companies with Goods at a meere nothing. . . .[69]

The traders could not understand this attitude, consumed as they were by the profit motive.

During competition then, the traders alternately wooed,

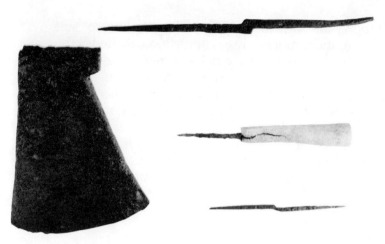

An axe head and trade awls. Both offset awls and axes became popular trade items with the Indians. The middle awl has been set in antler.

This photograph illustrates the variety in the trade process. The long piece of metal at the top of the picture is the handle from a bale of trade goods. The five cone-shaped articles are tinkling cones. The Indians attached the cones to the fringes of their garments where they made a pleasant jingling sound. The remaining item in the photograph is a fire steel handle. Both Indians and traders struck the steel with gun flints to create sparks. The accompanying sketch shows a complete fire steel.

This nearly complete bottle once held "Turlington's Balsom of Life." This popular medicine, used to treat common complaints, was composed of many varied items including nettle seeds, marsh mallows, and cloves.

Clay tobacco pipe stem and bowl fragments. Tobacco was a popular trade good, and was often given out to Indian trading chiefs during the pre-trade ceremonies. This made the pipe a sought after commodity.

cajoled and intimidated the Indians in an effort to obtain as many of their furs as possible. The Indians tended to remain loyal to the North West Company because it had first established contact with them. While they were anxious to trade with more than one company, they were careful to maintain contact with the company that could offer the most goods and services. The Chipewyans wisely showed a reluctance to change allegiance to a new trading concern for fear it would not return the following year. Fidler maintained this was part of the problem that had handicapped the Hudson's Bay Company when it tried to establish itself in the area in 1802. The Indians had expected the Company men to return after Turnor's visit in the 1790s:

> our telling them that we would return the same summer following with plenty of Goods & to build houses in their Country . . . but not our keeping to our word in that respect; it makes them dubious that we shall again abandon them to the mercy of the Canadian traders. . . .[70]

When they did not return, the Indians were left to depend on the Northwesters and, not unnaturally, distrusted the men from the Bay.

During the final phase of intense competition from 1815 to 1821, the Indians continued to operate in their own interest. A frustrated William Brown commented that the Indians were industrious while monopoly reigned in the Athabasca, but that opposition had "rendered them indolent and dissipated."[71] George Simpson observed how the Chipewyans endeavoured to use both companies to their advantage:

> they settle among themselves who are to join the French and who the English; the head of a numerous Family almost invariably attaches so many to one side and so many to the other, and individuals frequently take credit at each Fort and divide their hunts. . . .[72]

The intense competition, however, placed the Indians badly in debt: they did not trap enough furs to cover the cost of their fall outfits.

Simpson reported it was hopeless to expect them to pay their accounts.[73] In 1819, William Brown laid the blame for the diminished returns on "the enormous load of Indian Debts from last year."[74] In an effort to stimulate the Indians to make better hunts, Simpson reduced their debts by one half.[75] The costs to the Company were especially high because the Chipewyans preferred specific trade articles:

> The trade with the Chipewyans has always been considered very expensive . . . owing to their partiality to Bale Goods, they have been long accustomed to be indulged in this way, and for this only will they be industrious. . . .[76]

Guns were a very important trade item. The Indians used them in their provision hunts. This photograph shows a breech block and barrel from a pistol, a gun reserved for personal use.

A hunter could also obtain his supply of goods and then retire to his lands, effectively evading payment of his debt.

The problem of debt loads remained after the 1821 amalgamation. In 1822, the Company reduced debts by 40 percent.[77] This was not enough, however, and only reinforced the fact that the debt system was not profitable in the Athabasca. James Keith changed the system in 1823. He reduced the price of goods to compensate for discontinuing the practice of giving small gifts throughout the year. He did, however, continue the tradition of giving gifts of clothing to the Indians in the spring.[78] The new system brought a saving of £65 8s. 9d.[79] Although Keith failed to get away altogether from a system of credit,[80] he hoped that it would eventually be done away with.[81]

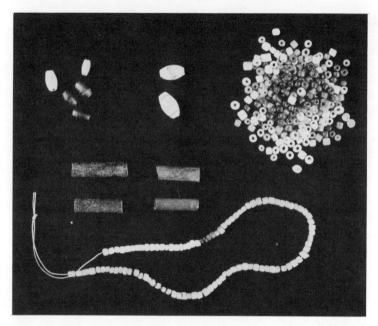

This photograph shows some of the many kinds of beads used in the Indian trade. In the top row at the left are glass trade beads of varying colours. The two beads in the centre of the top row are two large beads with floral designs. At the right and on the string at the bottom of the photograph can be seen small beads often called pony beads. They would not normally have been strung together. Finally, the four long beads are examples of tubular beads. To make these beads, the glass maker drew the molten glass into long tubes. When the glass had cooled, each tube was cut into varying lengths.

This axe was unearthed close to the fort site at Fort Chipewyan in Isobel and Noel (now deceased) Mackay's garden. This type of axe head was very common in the northwest from the late 1700s through the 1800s. It was hand forged from two pieces of metal.

Some modification of this plan had taken place by 1828. Simpson noted the changes:

> They are already become quite reconciled to the abandonment of the Credit system, our dealings with them will therefore be entirely confined to a barter trade in future: Liquor they never talk of now, and it is singular enough that those Indians, who but a few years ago were nearly unmanageable, from the bad habits contracted in the hottest opposition ever known in the Indian country. . . .[82]

In 1829 Alexander Stewart noted that the Indians found the new system to be satisfactory, being pleased at "finding themselves so rich in property."[83] The barter system was quite simple, and worked very well. John McLean described the system in use at Fort Chipewyan in 1833:

> Beaver is the standard according to which all other furs are rated; so many martens, so many foxes, & c., equal to one beaver. The trader, on receiving the Indian's hunt, proceeds to reckon it up according to this rule, giving the Indian a quill for each beaver; these quills are again exchanged at the counter for whatever article he wants.[84]

By that time, it would appear the system had recovered from the damage inflicted by the last frantic years of competition that had preceded the 1821 amalgamation.

From the moment a trader first arrived in the Athabasca district, he had one objective: to see to it that the Indians brought the maximum number of furs to the fort. He had little interest in the Indians' culture and lifestyle except for those areas that affected the fur trade. The fur traders assumed the Chipewyans would act according to the precepts of the European economic system. When it became clear to the traders that the Indians were not driven by the profit motive and did not necessarily engage in the wanton accumulation of material goods, they sought ways to increase the Indians' returns by exploiting aspects of their cultural traditions. Of these, the traders found participating in the pre-trade ceremonies and the giving of gifts to be the most successful. They were not averse to less pleasant methods, however, and sometimes intimidated or threatened the Chipewyans to get what they wanted.

For their part, the Indians did not simply fall in line with the traders' demands. They drove a hard bargain for their furs, and refused to trade for inferior trade goods. During periods of competition, the Indians reduced their fur output because fewer furs bought them the goods they required. They also showed no hesitation in trading only where they received the best treatment or a better deal. While competition gave the trading advantage to the Indians, monopoly gave it to the traders. It is little wonder then, that the traders fought so hard to secure a monopoly in the Athabasca.

Other factors, some of the more critical being disease, the death of a band member and the Indians' spiritual beliefs, also affected the hunt. The Indians carried no immunity to European diseases, and suffered terribly from the frequent epidemics. Their spiritual beliefs determined aspects of their behaviour, another factor the fur traders had difficulty accepting.

Many factors, then, affected the conditions under which trade was carried on. The convergence of European and Chipewyan cultures forced adjustments by both Indians and traders. For the traders, the adjustment was particularly critical during periods of competition. Under monopoly, they had less need to be accommodating.

6. MAKING THE ATHABASCA PAY: THE ECONOMICS OF A DISTRICT DEPOT

A profitable yield of furs at any trading post depended upon a number of factors. The dictates of fashion largely determined the market demand for beaver pelts. Not only the efficiency of Indian hunters, but their willingness to bring their furs to the fort, were important factors. Weather conditions could affect things as varied as transportation or the beaver population. It was the wintering partner's responsibility to choose the fort site, select and requisition his trade goods, and entice both the Indians and his men to engage in a profitable trade. Of all the variables affecting management's effort to ensure a successful trade, however, the most important was the trade environment of monopoly or competition.

It is within the framework of monopoly and competition, then, that the economic value of Fort Chipewyan and the Athabasca district can be determined. The Athabasca district provided a rich return in furs during the years monopoly prevailed but in times of competition the cost of obtaining furs increased to a point where the district was in danger of becoming a liability. As Innis pointed out,

> Both companies took advantage of monopoly departments to support the losses suffered in competitive areas. The Northwest [sic] Company had guarded the Athabasca department as a reserve of the best furs and as a monopoly but the effect of the competition was pronounced.[1]

Examining the Athabasca district as it swung between periods of monopoly and competition illustrates how having a rich fur-bearing district was not enough to ensure profitable returns.

The surviving documents for the period to 1821, particularly for the North West Company, are fragmentary. The wintering partners were careless about keeping track of their records, a fact noted in Ferdinand Wentzell's remarks to Roderick Mackenzie that the Athabasca accounts and journals, which were at Lac la Pluie in 1812, were carelessly strewn about the place.[2] Much of the information must then be gleaned from letters and journals that make only general references to the trade of the Athabasca district. These references often indicate the trend of the trade in the district, rather than referring directly to Fort Chipewyan. Still, enough information exists to draw an interesting picture of the area and Fort Chipewyan's existence during this important period of the fur trade.

The steady expansion of operations in the Athabasca district testifies to its importance. In 1786 four posts had been established: Peter Pond's fort on the Athabasca River, Laurent Leroux's post at the mouth of the Slave River, Cuthbert Grant's at the same place, and a provisions post on the Peace River.[3] By 1802, the North West Company had eighteen posts in the district, out of a total of 117 for the entire trade.[4] Almost one-fifth of the Company's entire work force was employed in the Athabasca district.[5] This totalled 207 of the Company's 1,058 employees. This rapid expansion can be attributed not only to the search for furs, but also to the competition of the XY Company. As well, Fort Chipewyan had the added burden of being the depot for the northern posts, and required extra men to transport goods and furs to the posts beyond.

It comes as no surprise, then, to note that the Company's single largest cost of all the expenses incurred in obtaining furs was the bill for its employees' wages. The men's wages varied depending on whether monopoly or competition held sway. Prior to 1800, the wages of middlemen, foremen, and steersmen were set between £20 and £42 (Tables 2 and 3).[6]

After the entry of rival firms, these North West Company employees received from £33 to £50 while their English rivals received from £16 to £20 (Tables 4 and 5).

TABLE 2   Athabasca Wage Scheme 1786

Year	Occupation	Livres	£ Sterling (Approximate)*
1786 NWC	Middlemen *(Milieux)*	500	20
	Foremen or Boatmen *(Devants)*	800	33
	Guide	1,000	42
	Clerks *(Commis)*	600-1,000	25-42
	Steersmen *(Gouvernail)*	700-800	30-33

Source: HBCA/PAM F.2/1, North West Company Post Journal, 1786, English River. Professor A.S. Morton has left a note on this document. He reasons that the journal is actually one kept at Pond's fort on the Athabasca River. Whether it is or not, the wage scales for English River and Athabasca were probably the same.

* The values and types of currency tend to be confusing. In Canada the French *livre* and the Spanish *dollare* were in use. The types of currency commonly mentioned were Canadian (or French) currency, Halifax currency, York currency, Grand Portage currency, and English sterling

Although Davidson says that Canadian and Halifax currency were the same, Rich states that Halifax currency was only used for accounting purposes. Certainly, these types were of less value than English sterling. The problem here is to make a *livre* correspond to a sterling value.

After 1796, according to Rich, the following values were accepted:
   1 sterling guinea = 21 shillings = 252 pence sterling value
   1 sterling guinea = 23s. 4d. = 280 pence Halifax value
   1 sterling guinea = 28 *livres* French currency
   5 shillings Halifax = 6 *livres* French currency
Therefore,
   60 pence Halifax = 6 *livres* French currency

10 pence Halifax = 1 *livre* French currency
If 1 sterling guinea = 28 *livres* French currency, then 252 pence sterling
= 28 *livres* French currency; and therefore, 9 pence sterling = 1 *livre* French
currency.

Davidson rates 7/8 *livre* = 1 shilling
Rich rates 5/6 *livre* = 1 shilling
Innis rates 1 *livre* = 1 shilling, Halifax currency
Pendergast rates 1 *livre* = .833 shillings and 1,000 *livres* = £41 13s. 4d.

Taking 5/6 or 7/8 *livre* to one shilling, the above conversion from *livres*
to £ sterling has been figured approximately. This conversion allows a
better comparison of the variation in wages throughout the period.

Grand Portage currency is explained by Gates (*Five Fur Traders of the
Northwest*, 94) as twelve units of G.P.C. equal £1 sterling. See 1799, Table 12.

York (New York) currency, according to Rich, rated a dollar to eight
shillings. Davidson says it was in use around Toronto and southern and
western districts of Upper Canada.

For a fuller account of currency, see:
E.E. Rich, ed., *Journal of Occurrences*, 186n.
G.C. Davidson, *The North West Company*, 202n.
H.A. Innis, *The Fur Trade*, 230n.
Pendergast, "The XY Company - 1798-1804" (Ph.D. dissertation, Ottawa,
1957), 120.

TABLE 3   Athabasca Wage Scheme 1795

Year	Occupation	Livres	£ Sterling (Approximate)
1795	Men	600-1,000	25-42
NWC	Guides	1,000-3,000	42-126
	Interpreters	1,000-3,000	42-126
	Clerks	100*-5,000	4-210

Source: G.C. Davidson, *The North West Company*, 234. He
quotes a North West partner in the Athabasca district, probably
at Fort Chipewyan, in 1795. Quoted in Masson, *Bourgeois*, vol.
1, 93.

As can be seen from Table 12, wages varied according to the ability and length of service.

Wentzell's statement of 1807 helps clarify this table:

> The wages allowed to a clerk at the expiration of a long term of seven years, which he has served for an apprentice for the sum of one hundred pounds for the whole term,† was formerly the reasonable salary of one hundred pounds per annum. . . .

* This figure may be in error, unless it applies to apprenticing clerks. It can reasonably be assumed that Athabasca salaries would be the highest of the districts. Cf., H.A. Innis, *The Fur Trade*, 238. This is true after 1821, until the Columbia district was established. Cf., R.H. Fleming, *Minutes of Council.*

†Thus, as an apprentice advanced in his experience, his wages increased accordingly. This explains the wide discrepancies that appear in Table 12.

TABLE 4   Athabasca Wage Scheme 1800

Year	Occupation	Livres	£ Sterling (Approximate)
1800 NWC	Foremen	1,200	50
	Steersmen	1,200	50
	Middlemen	800	33

Source: H.A. Innis, *The Fur Trade*, 239. In 1800, James Mackenzie records an interesting note on wages during competition on the Athabasca:

> Perronne [of the XY Company] asked him [a North West Company Canadian] how much wages he would ask to which Piché answered 700 livres with several other prerequisites of no great value per year. Here Perronne wisely reprimanded him . . . in exacting so little. . . . I trouve Piché que vous ete bien fou de demander si peu de Gages—Car pour un homme de votre Capacité on ne regardera pas 900 livres pour la première année et 1,000 pour la deuxième & pour toute autre chose vous serez haute comme le Bourgeouis. . . .

PAC. Journal of James Mackenzie, 5 July 1800.

TABLE 5   Athabasca Wage Scheme 1802

Year	Occupation	£ Sterling
1802 HBC	Foremen	20
	Steersmen	25
	Middlemen	16

Source: HBCA/PAM B.39/a/1, Nottingham House Journals, 7 August 1802. These Bay men were on a one-year trial engagement. Consequently, three middlemen demanded £18 each, an increase of £2 on their previous salary (HBCA/PAM B.39/1/1, 16 May 1803). The wages of the Bay men remained fairly stationary since more of them were demanding an increase to £18 each in 1805 (HBCA/PAM B.39/a/4, 23 May 1805). The man who remained inland in charge of Great Slave Lake during the summer of 1805 also was to receive £18.

At the close of the conflict, their wages fluctuated between £12 and £31 (Table 6). In 1806, the North West Company set a schedule for all departments under which canoemen received from £16 to £25 (Table 7).

TABLE 6   Athabasca Wage Scheme 1805

Year	Occupation	Livres	£ Sterling (Approximate)
1805 NWC	Guides	800	33
	Foremen	500-750	20-31
	Steersmen	500-750	20-31
	Middlemen	300-550	12-22

Source: H.A. Innis, *The Fur Trade*, 239.

TABLE 7   Athabasca Wage Scheme 1806

Year	Occupation	Livres	£ Sterling (Approximate)
1806 NWC	Foremen or Bowsmen	600	25
	Steersmen	600	25
	Middlemen	500	16

Source: W.S. Wallace, *Documents*, Minutes of North West Company, 1801-06, p. 213, 15 July 1806. Wentzell (in L.R. Masson, *Bourgeois*, vol. 1, p. 95, Wentzell's Letters, Forks, Mackenzie River, 27 March 1807) makes an interesting observation a year after this regulation had been approved:

> The prices of common men or Canadians are, by an established rule, never to exceed fifty or sixty pounds, being the highest, the lowest is twenty-five pounds, but few have these low prices.

A comment by Wentzell casts some doubt as to whether this scale was strictly adhered to in the Athabasca district. A year after the 1806 regulation had been approved, he noted that the "prices of common men or Canadians are, by an established rule, never to exceed fifty or sixty pounds, being the highest, the lowest is twenty-five pounds, but few have these low prices." At the height of the opposition with the Hudson's Bay Company in 1819, these wages were officially set at between £42 and £58 (Table 8). Once monopoly control returned with the amalgamation, wages fell: the Canadian employees received about 25 percent less, from £33 to £50, and the Europeans from £17 to £24 (Table 9). In 1823, the wages of Athabasca boat and canoemen were set between £19 and £24 (Tables 10 and 11).

They remained at this level until 1835.[7]

TABLE 8   Athabasca Wage Scheme 1819

Year	Occupation	Livres	£ Sterling (Approximate)
1819 NWC	Middlemen	1,000	42
	Bowsmen and Steersmen		
	(Bouts)	1,400	58
	Interpreters	1,600-2,000	66-83
	Clerks		150-200

Source: L.R. Masson, *Bourgeois*, vol. 1, pp. 123-24, Wentzell's Letters, Great Slave Lake, 5 April 1819. Wentzell said that some of the Hudson's Bay clerks were receiving as much as £300.

TABLE 9   Athabasca Wage Scheme 1822

Year	Occupation	Livres	£ Sterling (Approximate)
1822 HBC	**Canadian Scale**		
	Bowsmen and Steersmen	1,800	42
	Middlemen	800	33
	Guides	1,200	50
	Interpreters	up to 1,000	up to 42
	European Scale		
	Steersmen		24
	Bowsmen		20
	Middlemen		17
	Guides		up to 30

Source: R. Fleming, ed., *Minutes of Council*, p. 26, 24 July 1822, Resolutions 105-107; Athabasca and Lesser Slave Lake Districts.

TABLE 10   Athabasca Wage Scheme 1823

Year	Occupation	£ Sterling
1823 HBC	Steersmen	24
	Bowsmen	22
	Middlemen	19
	Guides	29
	Interpreters	up to 25
	Mechanics (inland)	up to 24

Source: R. Fleming, ed., *Minutes of Council,* p. 65, 1 July 1823, Resolution 1; Athabasca, McKenzies River, and Lesser Slave Lake Districts.

TABLE 11   Athabasca Wage Scheme 1825

Year	Occupation	£ Sterling
1825	Steersmen	24
	Bowsmen (canoe)	24
	Bowsmen	22
	Middlemen	19
	Guides	29
	Interpreters	15-25
	Mechanics (inland)	up to 24
	Boat Builders	up to 30

Source: R. Fleming, ed., *Minutes of Council,* pp. 117-18, 20 June 1825, Resolutions 78-81; Athabasca and New Caledonia Districts. These wage scales remained in effect until 1836. Cf., E.H. Oliver, ed., *The Canadian North-West, its early development and legislative records: Minutes of the Councils of the Red River Colony and the Northern Department of Rupert's Land,* PAC, no. 9, Ottawa, 1914-15, vol. 2, p. 749.

Monopoly, then, permitted at least partial wage control.[8] Other ways to decrease the Company's costs, however, were always being sought. The North West Company tried to increase efficiency and reduce costs by reducing the number of dependents at each post.[9] A great number of Indians had gathered about the posts during competition, attracted by the opportunity of getting trade goods more easily. The population list of 1822 reveals that there were 591 Chipewyans and 102 Crees at Fort Chipewyan, totalling 693 out of a total of 2,150 for the entire district.[10] In his 1823 report, Smith spoke of the attempt to disperse the Indians:

> the Elk River, Bark River in Clear Lake, the Lower parts of Peace River, and Fond du Lac Athabasca, has been alternately tried for this purpose but without answering expectations.[11]

He said that an attempt would be made to establish some of them at Hay River in the coming year.[12] Smith's endeavours were apparently to no avail since there were 593 Chipewyans and sixty Crees listed at Fort Chipewyan in 1824.[13]

James Keith, Chief Factor at Fort Chipewyan from 1823 to 1826, also tried to reduce the number of Indians at the fort by sending some to Hay River. Another group was encouraged to hunt furs around the western end of Great Slave Lake.[14] In 1826, he reported that some Indians had returned to the barren lands.[15] The number of Indians receiving advances at the Fort gradually declined: 128 Indians received outfits in 1825,[16] but only eighty-two in 1835.[17]

At the cessation of hostilities in 1821, Fort Chipewyan was also burdened with a surplus of fur traders and company men. The Athabasca district listed 330 men, in addition to the officers, in 1821-22.[18] The number of men decreased by about one-third during 1822, to 234. When the sixty-nine women, fifty-five boys, and seventy-four girls are added to the men, it makes a total of 432 European/Canadian dependents on the Athabasca trade.[19] In an effort to reduce the number of extra hands, 173 were sent to Upper and

Lower Canada. The report for the Athabasca district for 1823-24 lists only 118 people being supported at the Fort.[20] Fort Chipewyan, with lower living costs occasioned by the abundant fisheries, was being used as a residence for extra men not needed in Peace River.[21] The actual saving

> was a reduction from that of the preceding year of about £1,000 and a further saving of wages between Athabasca and McKenzies River of £3,000, exclusive of that arising from Equipt and subsistence say of 63 Clerks and men. . . .[22]

Throughout this period, the companies used the fisheries at Fort Chipewyan to sustain the men not needed for the trade.

Keith proposed reductions of sixty-three people for 1823-24, and an additional forty-six people for 1824-25.[23] The sixty-three people included one woman, sixteen girls, and twenty-nine children. Obviously, the policy was intended to reduce the number of children who could not make an economic contribution to the fort. Keith made no mention of where these children came from, who their parents were, or where they were sent. Keith felt that any further reduction in the number of men, however, would impair the efficiency of the trade. A change in the method of transportation to Mackenzie River posts did allow a further decrease of about twenty to thirty men in 1826.[24] According to the district report there were 111 people dependent on Fort Chipewyan in 1825-26, a number that included fifty-seven men, twenty women, eighteen children, and twenty-two other male dependents.[25] In 1827-28, Fort Chipewyan's population, excluding Indians, totalled seventy persons: twenty-four men, seventeen women, twenty-two children, and seven other male dependents.[26] In 1832 there were just eighteen men plus a number of women and children.[27]

A monopoly, then, was one of the most effective ways of controlling wage costs. After 1821, the Hudson's Bay Company could reduce the number of its employees, thus lowering the wage bill. The North West Company, confronted with two dangerous rivals within the space of a decade, never had the opportunity to reduce its manpower significantly in the Athabasca. Other methods had to be found. The main and possibly most successful attempt to control wage costs involved charging the employees high prices for goods at the posts.[28]

The Duke of Rochefoucault-Liancourt, travelling through the west in the late 1790s, noted that the price charged to the North West Company's employees for goods rose with each westward mile travelled:

> In Fort Detroit these articles are sold for three times their usual value in Montreal, in Fort Michillimakkinak four times dearer, at the great carrying place [Grand Portage] eight times, at Lake Winnipeg fifteen times; nay the agents fix the prices still higher at their will and pleasure.[29]

The practice of charging employees high prices for goods as a way of reducing wage costs remained constant throughout this period. George Simpson, writing in October of 1820, lamented that had he "a good stock of spirits it would work down their extravagant wages [as] the small quantity sold last night amounts to £43."[30] In November Simpson calculated that three-quarters of the men's wages could be recovered at the post if only the post stocked a sufficient quantity of rum. Simpson felt it was only good business to keep the goods on hand that the men wanted, relating as proof their willingness to pay a guinea a bottle for Madeira wine. There can be no doubt that both companies charged their employees high prices for goods to recover some of their prohibitive transportation costs and to control the amount of wages they had to pay in cash.[31]

In paying high prices for goods, many men piled up sizable debts with their companies. The Duke of Rochefoucault-Liancourt claimed that nine hundred men owed the North West Company more than ten or fifteen years pay.[32] Selkirk claimed the Northwesters charged their men eight dollars (forty-eight *livres*) for a quart of rum, while at Fort Wedderburn, the Hudson's Bay Company charged £18 a gallon. Apparently the North West Company prices at Fort Chipewyan were no cheaper.

It is interesting to note that in 1805 the debts of Athabasca River Department employees, who were paid on the same scale as those at Fort Chipewyan, exceeded their credits by 10,453 *livres*, two *sols*, of debts, or approximately £453 10s.[33] sterling. At Lac la Pluie, the eastern terminal for Athabasca brigades during the North West Company period, the men's debts exceeded their credits by 25,042 *livres*, one *sol*, which is about £1,043 sterling.[34] In 1819-20, 177 men were employed by the Hudson's Bay Company in the district.[35] Their wages totalled £8,134 10s., and their debts came to £1,712 1s. 2d. Thirty-nine men were free of debt. What is most interesting is that 119 Canadians had a total debt of 38,500 *livres*, fourteen *sols*.

The account book listing the men's wages and debts for 1821-22 reveals that, for the 324 Canadian men listed, wages totalled 357,829 *livres*, five *sols*, or approximately £21,740 sterling.[36] Their debts amount to 165,740 *livres* (about £9,944 sterling). A closer look at the accounts reveals the following:

	No. of Men
Excessive debts	44
Near Excessive debts	51
High debts	163
Minimal debts	50
Free of debts	15
	323

A man classified as having excessive debts had debts exceeding his annual wage. One with near excessive debts had a debt close to his annual pay. A man with high debts was one with a debt ranging from approximately 10 to 80 percent of his salary, while an employee with a minimal debt owed up to 10 percent of his salary. A large majority of the men, then, entered the coalition with substantial debts.

The practice of extending credit, or allowing an employee to carry debts, as a method of reducing wage costs did not always work in the employer's favour, however. If a man's debts were high, the employer would be reluctant to discharge him until they had been substantially reduced. During competition when men were in greater demand, companies were forced to rehire men they knew would simply continue increasing their extravagant debt load. This was obviously the situation at Fort Chipewyan in 1800:

> He [Courtois, a Canadian] engaged for four years which with 2 he was engaged before make him six - Tho' Contrary to my orders I gave this man his 4 phials in Goods as he owes a great deal and was in want of things which I did not like to add to his Acct - He promised to tell it to no body.[37]

Courtois apparently broke his promise since, five days later, another middleman was hired under similar conditions.[38] In 1816, John McGillivray summarized the problem of wages, debts and contracts:

> A number of our men's agreements expire this year. They will no doubt, according to custom, make it their province to extort as has been invariably the case on all similar occasions, I am sorry I cannot pass any high encomiums on them, the Generality of them being but a Set of *poor Dols* all the Good men were sent away by the Express orders and injunctions of the Agents, as they were in the habit of saving a little money, and few retained except drones and drivellers.[39]

George Simpson echoed this complaint in 1821, an indication that the problem was a persistent one:

> they know that we are dependent on their Services and exact such terms as they think proper: subordination is at an end . . . when he is asked to renew his engagement he not only insists on having all fines struck off his account but his Wages advanced about one third on some cases more.[40]

Management did not enjoy its employees having the upper hand.

With amalgamation, however, the Hudson's Bay Company not only held a monopoly on fur trading, but on labour as

116

well. It immediately began to streamline its operation assisted by George Simpson, as the governor of the new Northern Department. The policy of high wages and prices was one of the first to be discontinued. Simpson and the Council renewed

> the Contracts of a great many who are in debt and as an inducement to accept the terms, we have in all cases of doubtful Debts remitted of the old Debt in the ratio of 200 livres p. Annum for every 100 they relinquish of the price of the Post to which they are attached.[41]

Significantly, Simpson also reported that "Canadians not in Debt whose Engagements expire this Season have been discharged."[42] In 1825 Canadians with debts exceeding one thousand *livres* were induced to rehire for three years on the lower European pay scale.[43] The adjustment to the European wage and price scale made personnel management more efficient. In 1833, Chief Factor John Charles wrote in the Fort Chipewyan journal:

> Spoke to the men about Engaging; two declined and two others were so obliged to agree because we cannot furnish them with a passage outwards.[44]

Certainly this was a problem of less consequence than that of debt-ridden employees! In fact, there is little mention made of engagements in the journals, possibly indicating a satisfactory system.

Many employees continued, however, to incur debts, or have difficulty repaying old debts, after the amalgamation. The Fort Chipewyan account book for 1825-26 indicates that sixteen of the forty-two men posted there owed a total of £192 3s. 3d.[45] The 1830-31 account book lists forty-three men at Fort Chipewyan with a total debt of just over £594.[46] James Keith, in charge of Fort Chipewyan after 1822, favoured a continuation of the policy of wage control through prices of goods. In advocating the reestablishment of Berens House for the Crees, he said:

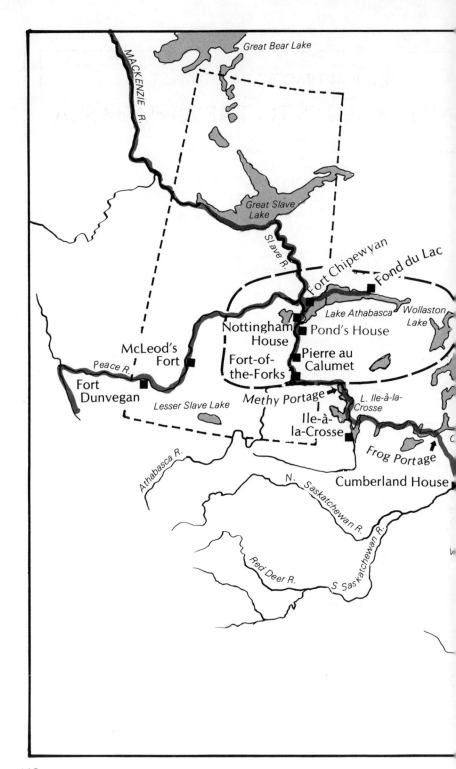

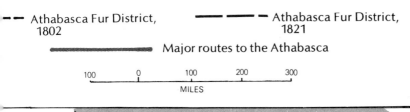

THE FUR TRADER'S NORTHWEST

AJOR ROUTES TO THE ATHABASCA

- - Athabasca Fur District,
    1802

— — — Athabasca Fur District,
    1821

Major routes to the Athabasca

100   0   100   200   300

MILES

HUDSON BAY

Churchill

Nelson R.

York Factory

Severn R.

Southern
dian Lake

James

Bay

edar
L.

Albany R.

Lake
Winnipeg

ke
anitoba

Fort William

Lake Superior

Red R.

The extra expence to be . . . the living & wages of an Engagé - an expence which in general estimation I am led to think is much over-rated and often the cause of nominal retrenchments productive of real sacrifices to the Concern, as it generally consists in the amount of Wages of the Individual employed, allowing the gain on the goods supplied him to more than compensate the cost of his subsistence . . . on these grounds am I led to believe that a reduction of men is not always a saving of expence much less productive of real advantage, as we often incur heavy risks & sometimes sustain serious losses for the sake of such nominal Petty savings. . . .[47]

The Hudson's Bay Company did not agree and, some time later, implemented a drastic policy in an attempt to curb the incurrence of debts by its employees:

in consequence of the heavy Debts of the Athabasca men it has been resolved at Norway House that whoever advances the men more than £3 the surplus is to be charged to the private account of the person advancing. . . .[48]

Clearly the prohibitive costs engendered by a vast transportation network and the isolated men's continued longing for liquor and other comforts made the cycle of high prices and high debts a difficult one to break.

What about the clerks' salaries? These men were vitally important to their companies and, during the North West Company's lifetime, were eligible for promotion to a partnership.[49] The companies tried to keep good clerks in the Athabasca because of the area's importance to the trade. Like their fellow employees, the clerks were not averse to bargaining from a position of strength: John McGillivray noted in 1815 that if the clerks were not enticed by salary increases to remain, "then we may as well deliver up the Country at once to our opponents."[50] Similarly, Colin Robertson stressed that the Athabasca district needed "every disposeable [sic] clerk" if the Hudson's Bay Company's trade was to be placed upon a sound footing.[51]

Table 3 shows a wide variation in clerks' salaries. As has been mentioned in a note accompanying the Table, the low figure of one hundred *livres* could have been a copying error, or it may apply to apprentice clerks.[52] Table 12 indicates the latter case is most probable. In 1807 (Table 13) the salaries had been reduced to a maximum of £100 for a first class clerk.[53] In 1819 clerks' salaries were raised to between £150 and £200 (Table 8).

TABLE 12

Arrangements of the Proprietors, clerks, interpreters, etc., of the North West Company in the Indian Departments, 1799 (the old Company) Athabasca

Year		G.P. Currency	£ Sterling
1799			
NWC	John Finlay, proprietor		
	Simon Fraser	1,200	100
	James Mackenzie	300	25
	Duncan Livingston	1,200	100
	John Stewart	240	20
	James Porter	480	40
	John Thompson	240	20
	James MacDougall	60	5
	G.F. Wentzell	240	20
	John Heinbrucks	500	41 6s. 0d.
		4,460	

Equipments and necessaries for 9 clerks at £20 . . . 2,160

Source: L.R. Masson, *Bourgeois*, vol. 1, p. 61.

TABLE 13   Clerks' Salaries (North West Company)

Year	Occupation	£ Sterling
1807 NWC	Clerks - First Year Second Year Third Year	60 80 100

Source: L.R. Masson, *Bourgeois*, vol. 1, p. 95. Wentzell adds:

For further wages we must depend upon success in trade and friends in power. Some enjoy an income of two hundred a year; such prices were only given because the times were pressing [i.e. opposition].

After the coalition of 1821, Simpson and the Committee disagreed on salaries for the Company's employees. The Governor and Committee proposed the following scale creating four classes of clerks:[54]

Class	£ Sterling
1st	150
2nd	120
3rd	100
4th	50-75

The London proposal acknowledged the many experienced clerks in the country who, the Committee felt, were worth more than newly appointed clerks.

Simpson, replying on behalf of the Council, stated that the scale was set "too high" and made the following counterproposal:[55]

Class	£ Sterling
1st	100
2nd	75
3rd	60
4th	40

Simpson probably carried his point when he said that several clerks had renewed their contracts on the above terms, "which seem to give entire satisfaction, and in most cases the advance on their former salaries is considerable. . . ."[56] The proposed scale is not much higher than the 1807 scale set by the North West Company (Table 13). Although the evidence is not conclusive, some doubt must be expressed about Simpson's contention that there would be complete satisfaction with the new arrangements. F. Wentzell, writing from Mackenzie River in 1824, affirmed the fact that "the North-West is now beginning to be ruled with an iron rod."[57]

In all fairness to Simpson and the Council, it must be noted that in a letter to the Governor and Committee, dated York Factory, 5 August 1822, Simpson told of what appears to be a wholesale dismissal of clerks for reasons of inexperience, age, drink, and dishonesty[58] Only a limited number remained in the Company's employ, an indication of Simpson's desire to operate the new concern on sound business principles. Clerks were to have a "respectable Education" and "capacity of body and mind" to assume more important postings. This dissatisfaction with its clerks also shows that the North West Company did have inefficient officers in its ranks, as John McGillivray had claimed in 1816. Although the evidence gives an incomplete picture, it is sufficient to suggest one reason for the dissension of the wintering partners that led to the collapse of the North West Company in the last Athabasca conflict[59]

The great distance separating the Athabasca region from most of the comforts of society was probably a key factor in determining personnel for the district. This is emphasized by the remarks of a Northwester in 1795:

> Gentlemen in Canada seem very fond of recommending their youthful friends to this country; but if they knew and considered the many disadvantages attending a young man in these distant regions they certainly would rather keep them at home. A Clerk here must serve a long time for a trifle, and after all in spite of abilities, friends or money, must

either remain dependent on the Company's pleasure, leave
the country or take the road to ruin.[60]

Alexander Mackenzie, a leading authority on the region at
the time, also had little good to say about the place:

> I am fully bent upon going down [i.e., from the Athabasca],
> for I think it unpardonable for any body to remain in this
> country who can leave it. What a pretty situation I am in
> this winter, starving and alone, without the power of doing
> myself or any body else any good.[61]

His attitude, that of a partner entitled to a full share in the
Company's profits, must certainly have been shared by many
of those clerks who, at a lesser salary, depended more and
more upon the favours of the Montreal agents for promotion.

After the coalition of the Canadian companies in 1804, the
opportunities for advancement became even more limited.
The letters of Ferdinand Wentzell reveal some of the
resentment one clerk harboured toward his employers after
the 1804 amalgamation. Wentzell spent most of his fur trade
career in the Athabasca district. In a lengthy dispatch to
Roderick Mackenzie, he revealed his perceptions of the road
to success:

> we [clerks] are flattered and feed ourselves upon the hope
> of once being admitted to a share in the Company, which,
> only friends and merit can procure us.[62]

Wentzell also mentioned later in the same letter that the
recent competition of the two companies had benefitted
those who were "roguish in private and dissemblers in
public." While these individuals were

> advanced to what their merits otherwise would not have
> entitled them, others, honest characters, let their abilities be
> ever so great . . . must think themselves happy in having
> the good fortune to gather the rags and be allowed the
> approaches of these *dissembling courtiers.*[63]

If Wentzell's accusation was correct, the Company's efficiency
must have suffered in the period between 1804 and the 1821
merger.

The North West Company, according to the later assessment of H.A. Innis,

> depended for its success on the individuality, self-reliance, and bargaining ability of each man. Surveillance from headquarters was impossible. It was adapted to secure from each partner the whole-hearted interest of the concern. The North West Company was designed to secure promotion which depended primarily on the ability of the trader to secure returns.[64]

Yet this apparently did not always apply at every level of the work force. Wentzell was clearly unhappy about both the established routes to promotion in the remote Athabasca district,[65] and the decreasing opportunities.

Assuming that there were few chances of promotion to partnership, what then happened to morale and efficiency? Both would most certainly decline, affecting the trader's success in securing returns. The North West Company thus had a problem not unlike that of its English rivals: a clerk on salary with little hope of promotion or better pay was not likely to pursue greater and greater returns. Three to five proprietors in the vast Athabasca territory could not maintain a close check on trading methods, accounts, and transportation costs. Clerks like Wentzell may well have resigned themselves to low pay but they also undoubtedly showed an equally limited concern for their employer's interests.

The cost of labour, inflated by the great expanse covered by the transportation network, comprised one of the major costs borne by the fur trading companies. The cost of labour rose even higher during times of competition when men were at a premium. The companies tried to control their labour costs by charging their employees high prices for goods at the posts. Despite their importance, however, wages and their control rank lower in importance than the production of furs in the overall picture. From an examination of the material available on fur returns and on outfits, Fort Chipewyan's importance to the fur trade can be determined.

The Hudson's Bay Company first monopolized the trade coming from the Athabasca country. The organization of Cree and Chipewyan middlemen initiated by James Knight in 1715 led to the establishment of Churchill as an important post.[66] Hearne reported that the trade between the Northern Indians (Chipewyans), who acted as traders, and the Far Indians (Dogribs and Copper) varied between six thousand and one thousand made beaver annually.[67] The disruption of this system by Canadian traders caused Hearne, at a later date, to estimate "the Hudson's Bay Company have now lost every shadow of a future trade from that quarter."[68] It is apparent, then, that the Hudson's Bay Company profited from the trade prior to the invasion of the pedlars.

The arrival of the pedlars drastically curtailed the Hudson's Bay Company's returns in the Athabasca. Near the end of the eighteenth century, Alexander Mackenzie exultantly noted that "yet from the manner they [Indians] are all distributed it will not injure the returns of the year in my opinion they will exceed those of the last which was the greatest we ever had."[69] Mackenzie was specifically referring to the returns of the Athabasca district. In 1792 Turnor had remarked:

> They [North West Company] carry from the North of Cumberland House between Forty and Fifty Thousand made Beaver every year . . . I have heard some of them declare that while they can draw the attention of the Honble Company's servants up the Sask-ash-a-wan or to Southern parts they can afford to oppose them at a trifling loss so long as they can keep the North to themselves.[70]

Table 14 reveals the number of packs taken from the north country in 1792. The furs, as Turnor noted, were mostly the highly prized beaver pelts. Clearly the Athabasca was a promising district.

The Athabasca-inspired enthusiasm continued. Alexander Henry (the Younger) concluded in 1800, "It is true, profits arise from the trade in other parts, eastward; but nothing in comparison to what we obtain from the Athabasca

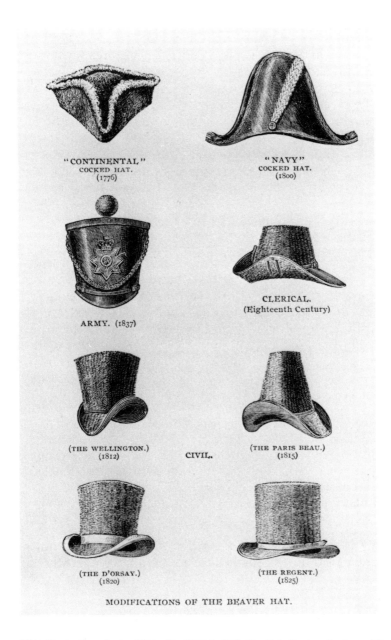

"CONTINENTAL"
COCKED HAT.
(1776)

"NAVY"
COCKED HAT.
(1800)

ARMY. (1837)

CLERICAL.
(Eighteenth Century)

(THE WELLINGTON.)
(1812)

CIVIL.

(THE PARIS BEAU.)
(1815)

(THE D'ORSAY.)
(1820)

(THE REGENT.)
(1825)

MODIFICATIONS OF THE BEAVER HAT.

This illustration, first published in 1892 in H.T. Martin's Castorologia; or The history and traditions of the Canadian beaver, *shows a variety of hat types that used beaver felt. (Public Archives of Canada, C-17338)*

TABLE 14   North West Company Returns 1792

Outfit not given	Returns No. of Packs	Estimated Value
Slave Lake	54	£3,240
Peace River	150	£9,000
Athapescow Lake	90	£5,400
Athapescow River	25	£1,500
		Total £19,140

Source: J.B. Tyrell, ed., *Journals*, 456, May 1792. Turnor reasoned that the expenses for this trade, after leaving Lake Superior (which included 25 percent advance on the "English Invoice" of trade goods), of goods and provisions did not exceed £700, plus wages of £500. He further estimated that for twenty thousand or more made beaver the pedlars' total expense to and from London would not be much more than £3,000.

TABLE 15   North West, Hudson's Bay and
XY Companies Returns 1800-06

1799-1800	Outfit		Returns	
	No. of Pieces	Men	No. of Packs	Estimated Value (£)
NW Co.	240	126	648	38,840
XY Co.	70	—	2	120

1801-02	Outfit		Returns	
	No. of Pieces	Men	No. of Packs	Estimated Value (£)
NW Co.	—	—	—	—
XY Co.	150*	—	10	600

1802-03	Outfit		Returns	
	No. of Pieces	Men	No. of Packs	Estimated Value (£)
NW Co.	700*	—	182	10,920
XY Co.	250*	—	31	1,860
HB Co.	100*	18	6 small bundles - 253 6 M Br	255

1803-04	Outfit		Returns	
	No. of Pieces	Men	No. of Packs	Estimated Value (£)
NW Co.	600*	195	315	18,900
XY Co.	250*	83	84	5,040
HB Co.	100*	—	M Br 463	463

1804-05	Outfit		Returns	
	No. of Pieces	Men	No. of Packs	Estimated Value (£)
NW Co.	600*	—	19 loaded canoes* (380)	22,800
XY Co.	275*	—	—	—
HB Co.	100*	9	M Br 164	164

Source: HBCA/PAM B.39/a/2, B.39/a/3, B.39/a/4, Nottingham
House Journals, 1801-06. The XY outfit for 1799-1800 is taken
from A.N. McLeod's journal in C.M. Gates, ed., *Five Fur
Traders*, 142, 17 December 1800.

* Indicates an estimated number of pieces.

country."[71] Innis contended that fully one-third of the Company's goods, equipment and provisions went to the Athabasca, Athabasca River and English River districts.

The outfits and returns for the years 1799 to 1805 summarized in Table 15 give a good indication of the fur trade's value and of the amount of goods needed to sustain it. Similarly, in 1809, twenty-six of the North West Company's total of eighty-eight canoes went to Fort Chipewyan, and twenty-six out of ninety-two went there in 1810.[72] Colin Robertson maintained that the North West Company calculated, "with reason, that Athabaska of itself, if managed with economy, which they can easily do if free from opposition, will yield a profit of £20,000 per annum."[73] Robertson continued, barely able to contain his enthusiasm, calling the Athabasca country "the richest in Furs that has as yet been discovered." Between 1808 and 1810, the total yearly returns for the North West Company averaged £102,925,[74] making the Athabasca's contribution quite a sizable part of the total returns. It is no wonder Robertson put forward such a strong case to the Hudson's Bay Company encouraging the Governor and Committee to try to establish a foothold in the Athabasca.

The North West Company's profits were maintained until 1819 (see Table 16). George Simpson claimed the returns for Fort Chipewyan averaged 120 packs of valuable beaver before the Bay men entered the territory.[75] William Brown, District Master at Fort Wedderburn, said, in his report, the returns averaged between seventy and 115 packs of fur. However, in 1819-20, Brown claimed that the Northwesters only took out ten packs of fur, and he guessed that they would only get twenty packs in 1820-21.[76] In his 1821 report, Simpson wrote:

> the returns would for several years to come, if the Indians resume their industrious habits be very considerable, as the country is now according to Indian report as it has been at any time within their recollection, so that there is still an ample harvest in Store for those who weather the Storm of Opposition.[77]

Could the North West Company, however, weather the "Storm of Opposition" intact? The answer became an increasingly clear no.

TABLE 16   **North West Company Profits 1814-18**

	Returns No. of Packs	£ Sterling Approximate value
1814*	380	22,800
1815†	400	24,000
1816‡	400	24,000
1817§	380	22,800
1818||	430	25,800

* L.R. Masson, *Bourgeois*, vol. 1, Wentzell's Letters, 114.

† Ibid., 117.

‡ PAC, MG E 1(1). Selkirk Papers, vol. 28, 8591, A. McLellan to J. McTavish, dated Bas de la Rivière, 20 July 1816.

§ L.R. Masson, *Bourgeois*, 119.

\|\| Ibid.

A major reason was the lack of preparedness on the part of the North West Company for opposition. Although Simon McGillivray (brother of William) had warned the North West agents in 1811 that the Bay men were preparing to invade the Athabasca and stressed the need to send in extra trade goods through Hudson Bay,[78] this advice seems to have been ignored. George Keith, obviously disgusted, remarked on the Company's lack of preparedness:

> At no previous period was the N.W. Co. provided to repel an opposition so disadvantageously. For several preceeding years the Country was starved in Goods, which fosters discontent among the Natives and our Outfit in Dry Goods was still less than usual and miserably deficient.[79]

The shortage of men and the desire of too many wintering officers to spend the summer at Fort William aggravated the situation.[80]

There were other indications too that the North West Company suffered from inefficient management. In 1816, all the required trade goods did not reach Lac la Pluie before the canoes had to depart for Fort Chipewyan. One trader reported that only ten canoes had made up the brigade, and had all the goods arrived, "more than double that number" would have made the trip.[81] In 1818, a different miscalculation hurt the trade:

> The outfit is however rather scanty for want of hands to take in the goods necessary for the trade. This has been occasioned by a bungling error of Mr. Rocheblave, the acting agent at Fort William. . . .[82]

William Brown also reported that "the Indians have already lost a great deal of the high opinion they had of them" because of the scarcity of trade goods in 1820 and 1821.[83]

Colin Robertson's extravagant display of trade goods and men, in effect, defeated the Northwesters at their own game. He fully realized that the key to winning the Athabasca trade lay in gaining the trade loyalties of the Indians. The 1814-15 expedition, for example, cost the Hudson's Bay Company well over £10,000.[84] In 1818 the North West Company failed to gets its brigades to Fort Chipewyan before those of the Hudson's Bay Company.[85] The result was a large defection of Indians from the North West Company's fort to Fort Wedderburn.[86] The North West canoes destined for posts beyond Fort Chipewyan failed to reach their quarters because of freeze-up.[87] John McTavish had to send twenty-five men to carry supplies to Fort Vermilion.[88]

Although the Northwesters were in earlier with the 1819-20 outfit, disaster of a different nature hampered the trade at Fort Chipewyan that season.[89] Measles and the whooping cough struck the Indian population in epidemic proportions in the Athabasca district, resulting in poor returns.[90] The presence of William Todd,[91] a surgeon, assisted the Hudson's Bay Company's campaign at Fort Wedderburn.

The evidence indicates that management was a major factor in the Athabasca contest. Colin Robertson had been correct when he said the North West Company could make a profit at Fort Chipewyan "if it was managed with economy, which they can easily do *when free from opposition.*"[92] His conviction that the Northwesters were "commercial monopolists," incapable of successfully trading against serious competition, proved correct.[93] He also succeeded in alienating the Indians from the North West Company. The second stage of the campaign, winning them to the English company, had not been completed when George Simpson arrived on the scene in 1820. The Indians, exploiting the favours of the companies, became independent of both.[94] The task of management after the 1821 amalgamation was to reorganize and recover from the damaging effects of competition.[95]

The trade at Fort Chipewyan, which became the headquarters of the amalgamated company, had not been as badly harmed as was feared. Simpson wrote in 1822 that

> The Indians . . . were in a state of great disorganization. . . . A system of moderate economy has been generally observed . . . things will in the course of a year or two revert to their original good order.[96]

Edward Smith, Chief Factor at Fort Chipewyan from 1821 to 1823, indicated that the new company would resemble its predecessors in its limited view of the Indians' trading participation:

> Altho there is a great concourse of Indians at this place still we have no complaint so far against them - they have strived to please and if it had not been for the ever restless and disappointed halfbreeds perhaps they would have done better.[97]

Smith maintained the Indians appeared ready to return to

"industrious habits."

Still, there were some problems. During the years of competition, most Indians were lured to the fort by the hope of more easily obtainable trade goods. One of the new management's principal concerns was to reduce the number of Indians living at the fort. The Company also found itself overburdened with servants in the Athabasca district.[98] The Peace River country had been largely depleted of furs, a condition caused by freemen and Iroquois.[99] The Beaver Indians were trapping beaver in the spring "when every female killed is then the loss of from 3 to 5 Beaver."[100] In contrast to the condition of the Peace River region, Smith described the Great Slave Lake area as better than a few years ago because the Indians had killed fewer beaver.[101] Finally, the confusion engendered by the final year or two of competition and the uncertainty of the outcome also complicated the post-1821 situation.[102]

With the return of monopoly, however, and the skills of men like George Simpson and James Keith, order soon returned to the Athabasca. Simpson's prediction made in 1820, that the district still held the promise of profits if monopoly control was restored, was proven true. During periods of competition, the cost of supplying the Indians with extra gifts and the reduced number of animals trapped because competition inflated their trading value combined to reduce a fort's returns. Some of the Indians were reluctant to accept the end of competition. About one-half of the Crees at the fort, "partly buoyed up & self deluded by the expectation of seeing *Strangers* had thought proper to decamp Southward."[103] There would be no return to the trading advantages the Indians had enjoyed under competition.

Tables 17, 18 and 19 show the beaver returns for the years 1821-35. The returns for outfits 1821-23 remained steady. James Keith was satisfied with the 1823 returns because the number of beaver taken from the Mackenzie River area increased.[104] He did note, however, that the 1823 outfit decreased "in value of about 10 p ct of the Returns of Outfit

TABLE 17   Beaver Returns 1821-25

Outfit	Returns				
	Ft. Chipewyan	G.S.L.	Peace River	Total	Approximate Value (£)
1821	68	47	68	183	10,980
1822	61	42	72	176	10,560
1823	50	31	90	171	10,260
1824	42	21	68	131	7,860
1825	47⅓	45⅓	72⅓	165	9,900
TOTAL	268	186	371	826	49,560
AVERAGE	53⅜	37	74	165	9,912

Source: HBCA/PAM B.39/a/29, p. 44, Fort Chipewyan Report on District, 1825-26. The approximate values are merely estimates. Cf., Appendix. The returns for each post are given in number of packs.

of 1822."[105] The slight drop in beaver for 1823 resulted from the failure of more than twenty of the best hunters of Great Slave Lake to make an appearance. The trade at Great Slave Lake also suffered because of battles between two Mackenzie River tribes.[106] The massacre of the traders at Fort St. John's in the autumn of 1823 also affected the returns.[107] The decrease in the packs collected at Fort Chipewyan was caused by Indians taking their trade to Fort Vermilion. The trade of these hunters had amounted to twenty-three packs in previous years.[108]

Throughout the district, the 1824 returns dropped sharply (see Table 20). All posts except Dunvegan showed decreases. The decline at Fort Vermilion was attributed to the absence of fourteen Chipewyans whose hunts in other years equalled the decrease.[109] The main reason for the smaller returns in 1824, however, proved to be an outbreak of hostilities between the Beaver Indians of Peace River and the

Chipewyans.[110] The hunting grounds of these two groups overlapped near the Chutes rapids on the Peace River. Keith understood that these Indians had clashed several times over the past twenty-five years. The Beaver Indians, being the more aggressive, usually dominated. Thus the Beavers' returns remained largely unaffected by these clashes, but the Chipewyan trade was "much affected and paralized [sic] thereby."[111]

TABLE 18   Beaver Returns 1826-33

Outfit	Returns				
	Ft. Chipewyan	G.S.L.	Peace River	Total	Approximate Value (£)
1826			not available		
1827	65	57	76	198	11,880
1828	63	55	81	199	11,940
1829	—	—	96	—	—
1830			not available		
1831	75	34	53	162	9,720
1832	87	43	87	217	13,020
1833	84	72	87	243	14,580

Source: HBCA/PAM B.39/a/26, 1828-29, B.39/a/27, 1831-32, B.39/a/28, 1831-34, B.39/a/29, Fort Chipewyan Post Journals, 1827-28.

Table 18 is not as accurate as Table 17 because the former table is taken from James Keith's accounts; Table 18 is taken from the daily journals which were not definite accountings.

According to William Brown, the furs taken by the North West Company prior to 1821 varied between seventy and 115 packs. Table 16 confirms his estimate since the Mackenzie River returns are included in these totals. Therefore, the district returned to a production not much below that before 1821. Simpson estimated Mackenzie River returns between 80 and 100 packs (E.E. Rich, ed., *Journal of Occurrences*, 393).

The late arrival of the outfit also had a negative effect on the returns. The brigades did not arrive at Fort Chipewyan until 8 October. The most severely affected posts were those at Peace River and Great Slave Lake as the brigades could not reach them by open water.[112] As a consequence, the Indians did not get away from the posts until after freeze-up. A substantial increase in marten prices, however, offset the declining returns from beaver. As of 1823, a pack of marten pelts was reputedly worth twice that of a beaver pack.[113]

James Keith summarized management's problems in his 1824-25 report:

> They are partly to be traced to the Declining & exhausted state of these Parts - the non-establishment of the R.M. [Rocky Mountain Portage] . . . no regular supplies for the Copper Indians usually attracted to Great Sl. Lake, the ferment & apprehension first excited among the natives by the murders at St. Johns . . . and aggravated by the late collision between the Chipewyan Indians . . . though the prime cause in my opinion is the late supplies in autumn which renders it impossible for the Indians to get in time to their respective hunting grounds. . . .[114]

At the close of his stay at Fort Chipewyan he concluded that these factors, along with depleted fur resources, were equally important in reducing returns. He could not, therefore, "furnish . . . conclusive Criterion whereby to Judge of the actually existing Resources of the District."[115] He recommended closer attention be paid to costs and conservation in place of the old maxim of making returns with little consideration given to the costs of production.[116] Keith's close attention to detail in management is evidenced by the careful accounts he kept at Fort Chipewyan. His comparison of the expenses of boat and canoe transportation from York Factory to Mackenzie River, for example, was

TABLE 19   Beaver Returns for Northern Department 1821-35

Outfit	1821	1822	1823	1824	1825	1
Athabasca	8,126	7,934	7,726	5,479	6,043	5
Western Caledonia (Columbia)	—	—	—	—	—	
Lesser Slave Lake	1,929	2,657	4,257	2,336	744	
Saskatchewan	2,924	2,834	3,543	3,286	6,453	5
B. River	—	1,292	—	—	—	
Fort Assiniboine	—	—	—	871	—	
English River	1,915	1,649	1,757	1,201	1,067	
Cumberland	391	434	272	303	397	
Swan River	583	497	523	644	432	
Upper Red River	45	197	140	—	—	
Lower Red River	93	126	30	37	80	
Winnipeg	179	57	44	123	76	
Lac la Pluie	652	502	826	735	501	
Norway House	145	169	138	7	26	
Nelson River	1,885	1,441	794	1,033	702	
Island Lake	697	577	352	187	157	
Oxford	—	—	—	—	—	
Severn	598	640	660	368	216	
York Factory	471	331	504	370	295	
Churchill	1,101	815	447	317	344	
Private Traders & Adventurers	82	—	—	182	86	
Mackenzie River	3,314	4,284	3,273	3,343	3,134	3,
TOTAL	25,130	26,436	25,286	20,822	20,873	17,

Source: PAC, MG 19 A 30. North West Papers, vol. 3, pt.3, C.N.

7	1828	1829	1830	1831	1832	1833	1834	1835
6	7,090	6,014	7,009	6,711	5,679	5,160	5,542	2,916
—	—	—	—	—	—	—	—	—
—	—	—	—	—	—	—	—	—
6	9,384	7,447	5,177	6,969	4,961	4,309	4,604	2,675
—	—	—	—	—	—	—	—	—
37	1,125	1,676	1,702	2,237	1,591	1,710	1,385	952
4	354	468	689	574	617	572	1,074	568
6	281	381	697	421	488	376	475	439
—	60	107	127	160	13	12	—	—
7	147	45	126	158	84	59	92	99
9	211	225	436	687	—	—	—	—
6	598	565	725	448	735	666	504	359
0	18	43	115	329	303	269	347	323
0	866	1,078	1,608	784	707	640	752	804
5	599	421	566	361	534	33	192	620
8	—	—	—	—	—	—	—	—
2	—	—	—	—	—	—	—	—
2	376	484	376	315	535	357	287	545
4	717	1,577	2,040	485	1,258	1,513	2,111	968
3	52	26	—	—	—	—	—	—
6	5,348	4,914	4,608	3,977	4,219	4,968	5,536	3,203
1	27,226	25,471	26,001	24,616	21,724	20,644	22,901	14,471

ection, Item 5.

undoubtedly appreciated by George Simpson. Efficiency in management paid off in 1826 with an increase in returns and a profit of £13,000.[117] In all likelihood, part of this profit accrued from the new system of careful trade methods Keith introduced.[118]

Traders, then, had some leeway in dealing with the local conditions that affected trade in their district. They could not, however, determine whether monopoly or competition held sway: that decision was taken elsewhere. Competition left a legacy in the Athabasca district that the 1821 amalgamation could not immediately erase. By the 1830s, however, Fort Chipewyan had lifted the legacy's mantle and settled into a long reign as the "Emporium of the North."

TABLE 20

Beaver Returns for Athabasca District Forts 1823-24

Post	1823	1824	Increase or Decrease
St. John's*	1,055	—	−1,055
Dunvegan	1,567	2,292	+ 725
Vermilion	2,575	1,291	−1,284
G.S. Lake	891	583	− 308
Chipewyan	1,740	1,367	− 373
TOTAL†	7,828	5,533	

Source: HBCA/PAM B.39/e/8, p. 21, Fort Chipewyan Report on District, 1824-25.

* The St. John's post was closed in retaliation for the killing of the traders there in the fall of 1823, as was Dunvegan. R. Fleming, ed., *Minutes of Council*, 104.

† Keith's totals differ from those in Table 19.

CONCLUSION

During the years between 1778 and 1835, the fur trade was firmly established in the Athabasca region. Its operations were directed from Fort Chipewyan, which became the focus of trade, transportation and the complex group of personal relationships engendered by the trade. Before 1821, life at Fort Chipewyan was characterized by the difficulty and turmoil associated with extending the fur industry into a new and isolated region, frequently in an environment charged with intense competition. Despite the unsettled circumstances, the value of the trade encouraged consistent development of trading practices which would be consolidated in the period following amalgamation of the North West Company and the Hudson's Bay Company in 1821.

The site of Fort Chipewyan was consistently central to the Athabasca fur trade because it proved to be the most accessible location for the interlocking requirements of fur production, provisioning, and transportation to and from the outside world. Thus Fort Chipewyan was more than a trading post; it was the important regional depot for receiving and transferring goods and men. Its significance was enhanced by the repeated seasonal hazards associated with the Athabasca environment, so that even the precise choice of the most advantageous location for Fort Chipewyan would not always maintain a perfect balance among accommodations, furs, supplies and food. The provisions forts along Peace River were prerequisites for a successful transportation system. The abundant fisheries at Fort Chipewyan provided a cheap source of food for the extra men required for the brigades. Nevertheless, there was an urgency in the movement of furs and trade goods each year because the season of open navigation differed for each northern river and lake.[1]

If access determined the location of Fort Chipewyan, its

business was complicated by a variety of environmental, market and organizational circumstances. Natural fluctuations were unpredictable. In 1795 and 1812, two serious epidemics of distemper evidently depleted the beaver population in the Athabasca district. Although the impact of the weather could be modified by improvements in transportation efficiency, nothing could overcome an early freeze-up which blocked the passage of canoes and boats. Far distant developments in fashion and technology were equally outside local control. The substitution of nutria[2] and silk in hat-making had a tremendous effect upon beaver values in the nineteenth century.[3] The range of ungovernable variables influencing the Athabasca fur trade increased the significance of local management and operations, and magnified the difference between conditions of monopoly and competition.

It was, for example, the responsibility of the North West Company wintering partner to choose the fort site, to select and requisition his trade goods, to entice the Indians to trade their valuable furs, and to get the men under his command to render a profitable return on their time. In a district as large as the Athabasca, these responsibilities were delegated, in part, to the clerks. First class clerks were expected to assume the management of lesser posts, such as those at Pierre au Calumet, Lake Claire, and Fond du Lac. Management of wages could be critically important. Prior to 1821, wages were tied in with the attempt of the North West Company to regulate the cost of obtaining furs. High wages meant high prices at a fort. By extending large credits to its employees, the North West Company was able to pay their salaries. The existing evidence, though by no means complete, shows that salaries were often consumed by purchases at a fort. This single example demonstrates the emphasis upon economy by which profits could be maximized by careful management.

Manpower was provided by imported *engagés* on the one hand, and Indian fur producers on the other. Life was exacting and laborious for the *engagés*. They worked hard and, when time permitted, they played hard. Although more research is required on the health and living conditions of the men, the records seem to indicate that the *engagés* were physically spent at a younger age than the officers. The Chipewyans provided furs as independent agents and transferred them to the trading companies through commercial transactions. The surviving records reveal something of the methods of trade devised and implemented in an effort to exploit the Chipewyan way of life. Even the merits of intercultural marriages according to the custom of the country, and the families which resulted, were debated in terms of their impact on the trade: the costs of dependents opposed to the benefits of enhanced provisioning and trade relations. Employed mainly as fur hunters, the Crees had a markedly different association with Fort Chipewyan as they traded provisions for liquor, a practice much less common among the Chipewyans.

The combination of their control of fur production with their status as independent traders made the Indians a principal focus of fur company attention. Understandably, the management of trading relations was easiest when one company controlled the contact, as did the North West Company from 1788 to 1799 and from 1806 to 1814, and the amalgamated Hudson's Bay Company after 1821. The competition which prevailed between 1800 and 1806 and particularly vigorously from 1815 to 1821 was anathema to successful trade. The Indians were perceived to become indolent when their needs were satisfied by extravagant gifts from rival companies. The fur companies divided their energies between the trade and attention to their competitors, at least to keep watch and often to sabotage each others' efforts with methods frequently culminating in violence. The North West spirit, exemplified in men like Archibald N. McLeod, the "Athabasca justice," and Samuel Black, was flamboyant and ruthless. The attitude of the Hudson's Bay Company long remained that of a company confident of its government charter, cautiously and carefully pursuing its trade according to accepted London business practices as though no competition existed.[4] In the final conflict, however, Colin Robertson, in a manner he described as more ostentatious and extravagant than that of any Hudson's Bay Company officer,[5] directed the Hudson's Bay Company campaign against the North West stronghold in the Athabasca. He employed tactics similar to the Northwesters', but even more efficiently and persistently, and the result was the collapse of their Athabasca eldorado.

Although the North West Company enjoyed a regional Athabasca monopoly through two separate decades before the 1821 amalgamation, it never featured the stability of the period following 1821. Before 1800, logistical problems of the trade still required solutions.[6] Before 1815, difficulties elsewhere prevented the North West Company from devising an efficient system to take full advantage of its Athabasca trade.[7] But the amalgamation of the two companies in 1821 allowed all hands to consolidate the lessons of the previous half century into a stable Athabasca trading system for which Fort Chipewyan remained the headquarters until new technologies of steam transport passed it by.

APPENDIX

The Value of Fur Packs

The basic unit for determining fur values is the "pack."[1] A pack weighed approximately ninety pounds, and its value depended upon the types of furs it contained and their current price. In 1800, James Mackenzie gave the contents of a fur pack as "44 Beaver Skins, 12 Otters, 5 Bears & 6 pichous (fishers)."[2] The number of beaver skins in a pack depended on the season in which the animals were trapped. Fall beaver skins were lighter than those trapped in the spring, as spring beaver still had the heavy winter coat. Fall beaver pelts weighed an average $1^3/_5$ pounds each, while spring beaver weighed approximately $2\frac{1}{2}$ pounds each. Thus a pack probably contained between thirty-five to sixty pelts.[3] The skins were packed pelt to pelt, hide to hide, to prevent damage to the hair. The less valuable skins, such as moose or summer beaver, covered the outside of the pack.[4]

Beaver was first graded, and then sold by weight. "Castor gras," or beaver where long wearing by an Indian had worn off the guard hair and left only the thick fur, was worth more than "castor sec," or parchment beaver. Parchment beaver still had the guard hair, and lacked the soft quality long wearing gave the castor gras. Another name for castor gras was "coat beaver," an indication of how it acquired its valued characteristics.

The price of parchment beaver went up from 19s. 9d. in 1784[5] to 31s. in 1819.[6] In 1824 the price was 36s. 1d.[7] and in 1837 the price was approximately 31s.[8] The rise in price per pound of beaver meant that pack values also increased. Around 1790 a pack of fur was estimated at £40.[9] In 1801, 148 packs from Upper English River were worth £4,581, or about £30 per pack.[10] In 1810, packs from north of Lake Winnipeg were worth £50 each, while Saskatchewan packs were £30 each.

Northern fur was usually worth more than that obtained in southern regions, because it would be thicker.[11]

Taking the given weight of beaver, and setting the price to be approximately £1 per pound, a pack's gross value would be between £80 and £100. In 1825, forty-two packs of fur were valued at £3,887 3s. 8d. at Fort Chipewyan, an average of £92 10s. 1d. per pack.[12] In 1826, the value of 47⅓ packs was £4,159 10s. 9d., or about £88 a pack.[13] Beaver, marten, and muskrat were the main furs taken in these years.

In 1824, George Simpson estimated the profit of a fur pack from the Columbia district at £60.[14] His estimates of the New Caledonia district packs were approximately £12,000 for 130 packs of furs or £92 a pack. Subtracting £3,000 for expenses, this left a profit of £9,000 or £69 a pack.[15] The Mackenzie River returns were estimated at 180 packs worth £13,000, or approximately £72 each.[16] Simpson did not say whether these figures were gross value or net profit. They were probably gross value because James Keith, in 1823, stated the value of a Mackenzie River pack to be £63 7s. 3d. A New Caledonia pack was worth £57 4s. 8d., and Athabasca packs (Fort Chipewyan) were valued at £64 7s. 4d. each.[17] In 1825, James Keith gave the following estimate of a pack as

> averaging £74 of which the actual cost would be nearly 11 p Cent would produce £66 clear gain.[18]

This information, then, gives reason to set an approximate pack value at £60 for the period of study.

NOTES

1. INTRODUCTION

1 Gordon C. Davidson, *The North West Company* (Berkeley: University of California Press, 1918), Appendix J, 280.

2 Mackenzie River became a separate district in 1823.

3 J.B. Tyrrell, ed., *Hearne and Turnor Journals* (Toronto: The Champlain Society, 1934), 398.

4 Ibid.

5 This point is known simply as "the rock" in Fort Chipewyan. On a visit to the local Hudson's Bay post one often hears the question, "Have you been up to 'the rock' today?".

6 Edwin E. Rich, *The History of the Hudson's Bay Company, 1670-1870*, vol. 2 (Toronto: McClelland and Stewart, 1960), 209.

7 Arthur S. Morton, *A History of the Canadian West to 1870-1871* (London: Thomas Nelson & Sons Ltd., 1939), 12. Harold A. Innis, *The Fur Trade in Canada* (Toronto: University of Toronto Press, 1962), 149.

8 Edwin E. Rich, *History of the Hudson's Bay Company*, vol. 1, 435-36.

9 W.S. Wallace, *The Pedlars from Quebec* (Toronto: The Ryerson Press, 1954), 9.

10 Arthur S. Morton, *History of the Canadian West*, 275.

11 W.S. Wallace, *Pedlars*, 15.

12 Frobisher is reported to have cleared over £9,000 in his fifth year in the interior. Arthur S. Morton, *History of the Canadian West*, 319.

13 Richard Glover, ed., *A Journey from Prince of Wales's Fort in Hudson's Bay to the Northern Ocean, 1769, 1770, 1771 and 1772* (Toronto: The Macmillan Company, 1958), 114.

14 J.B. Tyrrell, ed., *Journals*, 56.

15 Arthur S. Morton, *History of the Canadian West*, 289-90.

16 Richard Glover, ed., *David Thompson's Narrative* (Toronto: The Champlain Society, 1962), xvii.

17   Edwin E. Rich, *History of the Hudson's Bay Company,* vol. 2, 73.

18   Richard Glover, ed., *Journey,* xx-xxii.

19   Harold A. Innis, *Peter Pond, Fur Trader and Adventurer* (Toronto: Irwin & Gordon Ltd., 1930), 122-31.

20   Canada. *Annual Report of the Public Archives, 1890,* Ottawa, 1891, 52.

21   Ibid., 48, 50.

22   W.S. Wallace, *Pedlars,* 24.

23   Gordon C. Davidson, *The North West Company,* 14-15.

24   Letter from Alexander Mackenzie to agents of the North West Company, 1 February 1788, at Ile-à-la-Crosse, "Reminiscences" by Roderick Mackenzie in L.R. Masson, ed., *Les Bourgeois de la Compagnie du Nord-Ouest,* vol. 1 (Quebec: Imprimerie Générale, 1889), 24.

25   Ibid., 29.

26   Ibid.

27   Edwin E. Rich, *History of the Hudson's Bay Company,* vol. 2, 132.

28   J.B. Tyrrell, ed., *Journals,* 371-76.

29   A.G. Morice describes New Caledonia as being "that immense tract of land lying between the Coast Range and the Rocky Mountains, from $51°30'$ to $57°$ of latitude north." A.G. Morice, *The History of the Northern Interior of British Columbia; formerly New Caledonia (1660 to 1880)* (Toronto: William Briggs, 1905), 1.

30   Harold A. Innis, *The Fur Trade,* 245.

31   Edwin E. Rich, *History of the Hudson's Bay Company,* vol. 2, 140.

32   Richard Glover, ed., *Thompson's Narrative,* xx.

33   Ibid., xxi.

34   Edwin E. Rich, *History of the Hudson's Bay Company,* vol. 2, 142-43.

35   Ibid., 144.

36   Professors Rich and Glover differ in their interpretation of Colen's views. Rich states that Colen's chief concern was York and its trade while Glover says that Colen wanted to enter the Athabasca through setting up trade posts on the way. Cf.,

Edwin E. Rich, *History of the Hudson's Bay Company,* vol. 2, 142-54, and Richard Glover, ed., *Thompson's Narrative,* xxvii-xxxix.

37 Edwin E. Rich, *History of the Hudson's Bay Company,* vol. 2, 145.

38 An excellent account of Ross is given in J.B. Tyrrell, ed., *Journals,* Appendix C, 598 ff. His first name is spelled Malchom by Tyrrell and Rich. Glover maintains that the normal spelling of his name in the journals was Malcolm. Cf., Richard Glover, ed., *Journey,* xviiin.

39 Ibid., xxv.

40 Located at the junction of the Reindeer and Churchill rivers. Richard Glover, ed., *Thompson's Narrative,* xxx.

41 Ibid., xxvi-xxvii.

42 Arthur S. Morton, *History of the Canadian West,* 453.

43 Hudson's Bay Company Archives, Public Archives of Manitoba (hereafter HBCA/PAM) B.39/a/1, Nottingham House Journals.

44 Quoted in Edwin E. Rich, *History of the Hudson's Bay Company,* vol. 2, 256-57.

45 Arthur S. Morton, *History of the Canadian West,* 509.

46 Edwin E. Rich, *History of the Hudson's Bay Company,* vol. 2, 215.

47 Arthur S. Morton, *History of the Canadian West,* 510.

48 Ibid.

49 L.R. Masson, *Bourgeois,* vol. 1, 76-77.

50 Canada. *Annual Report of the Canadian Archives, 1892,* Ottawa, 136-37.

51 HBCA/PAM B.39/a/1, Nottingham House Journals.

52 Arthur S. Morton, *History of the Canadian West,* 508. Cf. Edwin E. Rich, *History of the Hudson's Bay Company,* vol. 2, 273-74.

53 Arthur S. Morton, *History of the Canadian West,* 508.

54 Edwin E. Rich, *History of the Hudson's Bay Company,* vol. 2, 274.

55 Ibid., 170-71.

56 Harold A. Innis, *The Fur Trade,* 278.

57 Edwin E. Rich, *History of the Hudson's Bay Company,* vol. 2, 259.

58   Ibid., 262.

59   Ibid., 263.

60   Ibid., 264.

61   George Wollaston's proposals, which came near to being implemented, were to pursue a timber trade on the Bay, accompanied with a withdrawal from the fur trade. See, Edwin E. Rich, ed., *Colin Robertson's Correspondence Book, September, 1817 to September, 1822*, vol. 2 (Toronto: The Champlain Society, 1939), xxix-xxx.

62   Ibid., xxi.

63   Ibid., xxii.

64   Edwin E. Rich, *History of the Hudson's Bay Company*, vol. 2, 265.

65   Edwin E. Rich, ed., *Robertson's Correspondence*, xxxvii.

66   Edwin E. Rich, *History of the Hudson's Bay Company*, vol. 2, 286.

67   Quoted in Edwin E. Rich, ed., *Robertson's Correspondence*, xxxii.

68   Edwin E. Rich, *History of the Hudson's Bay Company*, vol. 2, 316.

2. THE FORTS: THEIR LOCATIONS AND STRUCTURES

1   Richard Glover, ed., *Thompson's Narrative*, xxvi.

2   J.B. Tyrrell, ed., *Journals*, 394.

3   Guy H. Blanchet, "Emporium of the North," *The Beaver* (March 1946): 32.

4   I am indebted to Mr. Peter Nortcliffe, formerly the Forestry officer at Embarras Ranger Station, for this information.

5   John W. Garvin, ed., *Voyages from Montreal on the River St. Lawrence through the Continent of North America to the Frozen and Pacific Oceans in the years 1789 and 1793 with a Preliminary Account of the Rise, Progress, and Present State of the Fur Trade of that Country by Alexander Mackenzie* (Toronto: The Radisson Society of Canada Ltd., 1927), 246.

6   The voyageurs 'tracked' a canoe by pulling it with a rope fastened to the bow of the vessel. Tracking occurred most often in places of swift or shallow water.

7   Arthur S. Morton, *History of the Canadian West*, 295.

8   J.B. Tyrrell, ed., *Journals*, 455.

9   Quoted in L.J. Burpee, *The Search for the Western Sea: The Story of the Exploration of Northwestern America* (London: Alston Rivers, Ltd., 1908), 583.

10 Harold A. Innis, *Peter Pond*, 82.

11 In his journal, Philip Turnor noted the trip to Hudson Bay was a difficult one for the Indians. See J.B. Tyrrell, ed., *Journals*, 450. Morton mentioned the trade route followed the Churchill River. See Arthur S. Morton, *History of the Canadian West*, 289.

12 John W. Garvin, ed., *Voyages*, 20.

13 Ibid., 94.

14 Harold A. Innis, *Peter Pond*, 27.

15 John W. Garvin, ed., *Voyages*, 138-39, 141; L.R. Masson, *Bourgeois*, vol. 1, 30.

16 J.N. Wallace, *The Wintering Partners on Peace River, from the Earliest Records to the Union in 1821* (Ottawa: Thorburn and Abbott, 1929), 18.

17 L.R. Masson, *Bourgeois*, vol. 1, 25.

18 Ibid., 27.

19 Lake Athabasca is on the dividing line between the Canadian Shield and the Great Central Plain. There is a contrast between the barren rocky appearance of the north shore and the sandy forested south shore east of the Athabasca River delta.

20 L.R. Masson, *Bourgeois*, vol. 1, 27.

21 Witness, for example, his rediscovery of the old Kaministiquia water route from Lake Superior to Lac la Pluie. See L.R. Masson, *Bourgeois*, vol. 1, 46.

22 In correct geographical terms, the Slave River begins where the Rocher and Peace rivers merge.

23 J.B. Tyrrell, ed., *Journals*, 448-49.

24 HBCA/PAM B.39/e/3, p. 20, Fort Chipewyan Report on District, 1820-21.

25 Edwin E. Rich, ed., *Journal of Occurrences in the Athabasca Department by George Simpson, 1820 and 1821, and Report*

(London: Hudson's Bay Record Society, 1938), Appendix A, 414.

26 HBCA/PAM B.39/a/1, Nottingham House Journals, 1802-03, 18 September 1802.

27 McGill University, Masson Collection (hereafter MUMC). Journal of James Mackenzie, 16 April 1800.

28 HBCA/PAM B.39/a/3, Nottingham House Journals, 18 September 1803.

29 MUMC. Journal of James Mackenzie, 22 May 1800. The present Bustard Island is about eighteen miles east of Fort Chipewyan. The Bustard Island to which Mackenzie referred is probably Goose Island. It would be unreasonable, as well as hazardous, for canoes to cross to the present-day Bustard Island. Mackenzie referred to Big Island as Bustard Island, 23 August 1800.

30 Arthur S. Morton, *History of the Canadian West*, 510. The opposition could have reached the Athabasca country in 1799, however, since Mackenzie said, on 10 August, "the Potties arrived from the Peace River." It seems unlikely that the XY Company penetrated into Peace River by way of Lesser Slave Lake.

31 MUMC. Journal of James Mackenzie, 24 August 1800.

32 Ibid., 22 May 1800. This Pointe au Sable was probably the sandy point which is now referred to as Pointe des Morts by the old-timers (see map). Lefroy said, "The prettiest point in the neighbourhood is called the Pointe des Morts from the burial ground which is placed there." See G. Stanley, ed., *In Search of the Magnetic North* (Toronto: The MacMillan Company, 1955,) 85.

33 MUMC. Journal of James Mackenzie, 23 May 1800.

34 HBCA/PAM B.39/a/1, Nottingham House Journals, 22 September 1802.

35 Ibid., 23 April 1803.

36 Ibid., 10 May 1803; B.39/a/4, 22 April 1805.

37 Ibid., B.39/a/3, 18 September 1803.

38 Ibid., 13 November 1803.

39 Ibid., B.39/a/4, 3 August 1804. Fidler and Thomas Swain, accompanied by eight men in two canoes, comprised the whole of the Athabasca expedition for 1804-05.

40 Ibid., B.39/a/5a, Nottingham House Journals, 9 June 1806.

41 Edwin E. Rich, ed., *Journal of Occurrences*, Appendix A, 426.

42 HBCA/PAM B.39/e/3, p. 21, Fort Chipewyan Report on District, 1820-21.

43 Edwin E. Rich, ed., *Journal of Occurrences*, 360, 361.

44 Journal of Malchom Ross, 25 August 1791, in J.B. Tyrrell, ed., *Journals*, 442n.

45 MUMC. Journal of James Mackenzie, 16 April 1800.

46 Ibid.

47 Ibid.

48 For an excellent description of this method of building see Marius Barbeau, "The House That Mac Built," *The Beaver*, (December 1945): 10-13. Grace Lee Nute's *The Voyageurs Highway* (St. Paul: The Minnesota Historical Society, 1941), Appendix B, contains a copy of a description of the technique by Reverend Sherman Hall in 1832.

49 HBCA/PAM B.39/e/6, Fort Chipewyan Report on District, 1823-24.

50 Henry Lefroy, 25 December 1843, in G. Stanley, ed., *In Search of the Magnetic North*, 84.

51 HBCA/PAM B.39/e/3, p. 20, Fort Chipewyan Report on District, 1820-21. Brown gives the dimensions of Fort Wedderburn as 160 yards square.

52 Ibid. The store was in need of repair in 1832; HBCA/PAM B.39/a/28, 29 February 1832.

53 Ibid.

54 Ibid.

55 Henry Lefroy, 13 December 1843, in G. Stanley, ed., *In Search of the Magnetic North*, 66-67.

56 George Back, *Narrative of The Arctic Land Expedition To The Mouth of The Great Fish River, and Along The Shores of The Arctic Ocean, in the Years 1833, 1834, and 1835* (London: John Murray,

1836), 205, 5 November 1833.

57   Journal kept at Fort Chipewyan (manuscript copy), in possession of the Provincial Library, Edmonton, Alberta (hereafter Fort Chipewyan Journal, Alberta Provincial Library), 30 August 1823.

58   Ibid., 2 July 1823.

59   Grace Lee Nute, *The Voyageurs Highway*, 57.

60   HBCA/PAM B.39/a/29, Fort Chipewyan Post Journals, 8 July 1833.

61   Ibid., 11 July 1833.

62   HBCA/PAM B.39/e/3, p. 20, Fort Chipewyan Report on District, 1820-21.

63   Fort Chipewyan Journal, Alberta Provincial Library, 28 April, 16 October, 24 November 1823.

64   Ibid., 9 July 1822.

65   Ibid., 3 May 1824.

66   HBCA/PAM B.39/a/28, Fort Chipewyan Post Journals, 3 May 1832.

67   Ibid., HBCA/PAM B.39/a/27, 5 May 1828.

68   Ibid., 22 June, 2 July 1828.

69   Ibid., 30 September 1828. Generally summer was an ideal time for building construction. The amount of progress, however, depended upon the initiative of the summer manager. Undoubtedly the failure of gardens can also be attributed, at least partly, to the lack of attention by the post manager.

70   Ibid., 3 October 1828.

71   HBCA/PAM B.39/a/29, 9 October 1832.

72   Ibid., 5 April 1833.

73   HBCA/PAM B.39/a/28, 5 April 1832.

74   HBCA/PAM B.39/a/29, 25 March 1834.

75   MUMC. Journal of James Mackenzie, 28 August 1799.

76   Ibid., 16 August 1799; Fort Chipewyan Journal, Alberta Provincial Library, 11 November, 13 November, 5 September 1823.

77 G. Stanley, ed., *In Search of the Magnetic North*, 84.

78 Ibid., 94

79 Richard Glover, ed., *Thompson's Narrative*, 297.

80 MUMC. Journal of James Mackenzie, 21 December 1799.

81 HBCA/PAM B.39/a/27, Fort Chipewyan Post Journals, 1828-29, 7 April 1829.

3. THE PROBLEMS OF TRANSPORTATION AND PROVISION SUPPLY

1 Edwin E. Rich, *History of the Hudson's Bay Company*, vol. 2, 76.

2 Edwin E. Rich, ed., *Cumberland House Journals and Inland Journals, 1775-1782, Second Series, 1779-1782* (London: The Hudson's Bay Record Society, 1952), 5.

3 John W. Garvin, ed., *Voyages*, 20.

4 Edwin E. Rich, ed., *Cumberland House Journals*, 5.

5 The word "provisions" is taken to mean the food required for maintaining the fort and its brigades.

6 L.R. Masson, *Bourgeois*, vol. 1, 24, 34.

7 Harold A. Innis, *Peter Pond*, 87; Vilhjalmur Stefansson, *The Fat of the Land* (New York: The Macmillan Company, 1956), 180. This view is also taken by Arthur S. Morton in *History of the Canadian West*, 113.

8 Harold A. Innis, *Peter Pond*, 87.

9 L.R. Masson, *Bourgeois*, vol. 1, 24. A. Mackenzie to Agents of the North West Company, dated Ile-à-la-Crosse, 1 February 1788.

10 Ibid., 27.

11 John W. Garvin, ed., *Voyages*, 94.

12 J.B. Tyrrell, ed., *Journals*, 454.

13 HBCA/PAM B.39/e/3, p. 6, Fort Chipewyan Report on District, 1820-21. A traineaux, or traine, was a sledge about seven to eight feet in length constructed of birch. The front end was turned up so it could easily pass over the ice and snow, and was usually pulled by dogs. Cf., Charles M. Gates, ed., *Five*

Fur Traders of the Northwest, being the narrative of Peter Pond and the diaries of John Macdonell, Archibald N. McLeod, Hugh Faries and Thomas Connor (St. Paul: Minnesota Historical Society, 1965), 219n.

14 HBCA/PAM B.39/a/15, Fort Chipewyan Post Journals, 1819-20, 3 November 1819.

15 HBCA/PAM B.39/a/29, Fort Chipewyan Post Journals, 1831-34, 22 November 1832, 15 November 1833.

16 HBCA/PAM B.39/a/4, Nottingham House Journals, 17 January 1805.

17 J.B. Tyrrell, ed., *Journals*, 455.

18 Richard Glover, ed., *Thompson's Narrative*, 61.

19 L.R. Masson, *Bourgeois*, vol. 1, 28.

20 Richard Glover, ed., *Thompson's Narrative*, 94.

21 HBCA/PAM B.39/e/3, p. 8, Fort Chipewyan Report on District, 1820-21.

22 HBCA/PAM B.39/a/29, Fort Chipewyan Post Journals, 1831-34, 19 January 1833.

23 HBCA/PAM B.39/e/3, p. 7, Fort Chipewyan Report on District, 1820-21.

24 J.B. Tyrrell, ed., *Journals*, 455.

25 HBCA/PAM B.39/a/1, Nottingham House Journals, 8 March 1803.

26 Ibid., 6 May 1805.

27 J.B. Tyrrell, ed., *Journals*, 454.

28 George Back, *Narrative*, 80-81.

29 William K. Lamb, ed., *Sixteen Years in Indian Country, The Journal of Daniel Williams Harmon, 1800-1816* (Toronto: The Macmillan Company, 1957), 116; Edwin E. Rich, ed., *Journal of Occurrences*, 58, 283, 341.

30 Alfred C. Garrioch, *The Far and Furry North: A Story of Life and Love and Travel in the Days of the Hudson's Bay Company* (Winnipeg: Douglass-McIntyre Limited, 1925), 165. Garrioch was a grandson of Colin Campbell, a clerk and later a Chief Factor in the Athabasca district in the first half of the

nineteenth century.

31 John W. Garvin, ed., *Voyages*, 246.

32 J.B. Tyrrell, ed., *Journals*, 397.

33 HBCA/PAM B.39/a/3, Nottingham House Journals, 1803-04, 10 October 1803.

34 Ibid., 16 September 1803.

35 Ibid., B.39/a/5, 11 September 1805. Fidler's garden was destroyed by North West Company men in 1805.

36 Edwin E. Rich, ed., *Journal of Occurrences*, 364.

37 Ibid., 379.

38 Ibid., 3 June 1823; HBCA/PAM B.39/a/29, Fort Chipewyan Post Journals, 1831-34, 1 June 1832.

39 John Franklin, *Narrative of a Second Expedition to the Shores of the Polar Sea in the Years 1825, 1826, and 1827 Including an Account of the Progress of a Detachment to the Eastward, by John Richardson* (London: John Murray, 1828), 305.

40 Ibid., 307.

41 HBCA/PAM B.39/a/29, Fort Chipewyan Post Journals, 1831-34, 28 September 1833. See also George Back, *Narrative*, 464-65.

42 HBCA/PAM B.39/a/28, Fort Chipewyan Post Journals, 1831-32, 3 May 1832.

43 Ibid., 27 December 1832.

44 MUMC. Journal of James Mackenzie, 31 July 1800.

45 Ibid., 20 November 1799.

46 HBCA/PAM B.39/e/9, p. 8, Fort Chipewyan Report on District, 1825-26. See also HBCA/PAM B.39/e/8, p. 27, Fort Chipewyan Report on District, 1824-25, for Keith's calculation of the daily expenses of feeding each person:
Officers' mess: 1s. 2d.
Officers' families: 2⅔d.
Engagés: 4d.
Engagés' families: 1⅔d.

47 MUMC. Journal of James Mackenzie, 4 December 1800.

48 J. Richardson's Zoological Notes in George Back, *Narrative*, 519.

49 Ibid., 521.

50 Fort Chipewyan Journal, Alberta Provincial Library, 19 November 1823.

51 Ibid., 17 January, 24 January 1824.

52 R. King, *Narrative of a Journey to the Shores of the Arctic Ocean, in 1833, 1834, and 1835, under the Command of Captain Back, R.N.*, vol. 1 (London: R. Bentley, 1836), 152.

53 Charles M. Gates, ed., *Five Fur Traders*, 155n.

54 Ibid.

55 R. King, *Narrative of a Journey*, vol. 1, 152.

56 Ibid., 197. See also G. Stanley, ed., *In Search of the Magnetic North*, 69.

57 G. Stanley, ed., *In Search of the Magnetic North*, 69.

58 Caspar Whitney, *On Snow-Shoes to the Barren Grounds* (London: Osgood, McIlvaine & Co., 1896), 55.

59 James Alton James, *The First Scientific Exploration of Russian America and the Purchase of Alaska* (Chicago: Northwestern University, 1942), 85.

60 HBCA/PAM B.39/e/8, p. 27, Fort Chipewyan Report on District, 1824-25.

61 George Back, *Narrative*, 464, May 1834.

62 Ibid., 465, 23 May 1834. See also R. King, *Narrative of a Journey*, vol. 2, 212, 10 June 1834. Lefroy reported half a dozen head in 1843, see G. Stanley, ed., *In Search of the Magnetic North*, 85.

63 HBCA/PAM B.39/e/3, p. 6, Fort Chipewyan Report on District, 1820-21.

64 Edwin E. Rich, ed., *Journal of Occurrences*, 319, 23 April 1821.

65 Fort Chipewyan Journal, Alberta Provincial Library, 26 June 1822.

66 HBCA/PAM B.39/a/5a, Nottingham House Journals, 24 November 1805.

67 HBCA/PAM B. 39/a/4, Nottingham House Journals, 23 October, 9 December, 15 December 1804.

68 HBCA/PAM B.39/a/28, Fort Chipewyan Post Journals, 24 April 1832.

69 Richard Glover, ed., *Thompson's Narrative*, 397.

70 J. Dewey Soper, "History, Range and Home Life of the Northern Bison," *Ecological Monographs* 2, no. 4 (October 1941): 347-412.

71 Richard Glover, ed., *Thompson's Narrative*, 84 and 85.

72 Ibid., 83.

73 Richard Glover, ed., *Journey*, 182-83.

74 Richard Glover, ed., *Thompson's Narrative*, 83.

75 Richard Glover, ed., *Journey*, 163, 182.

76 Ibid., 163.

77 Ibid., 162.

78 Fort Chipewyan Journal, Alberta Provincial Library, 2 February 1823.

79 Ibid., 14 January 1824; 29 December 1822.

80 Ibid., 25 December 1822.

81 Ibid., 1 April 1823.

82 William K. Lamb, ed., *Sixteen Years in Indian Country*, 261.

83 Fort Chipewyan Journal, Alberta Provincial Library, 27 November 1823.

84 Ibid., 17 November 1823.

85 HBCA/PAM B.39/a/1, Nottingham House Journals, 27 December 1802.

86 William K. Lamb, ed., *Sixteen Years in Indian Country*, 147.

87 HBCA/PAM B.39/a/3, Nottingham House Journals, 20 May 1804.

88 Fort Chipewyan Journal, Alberta Provincial Library, 4 June 1823.

89 Ibid., 6 March 1823.

90 Ibid., 24 July 1823.

91 Ibid., 30 May 1823.

92 John W. Garvin, ed., *Voyages*, 125n.

93   Richard Glover, ed., *Thompson's Narrative*, 84.

94   Vilhjalmur Stefansson, *The Fat of the Land*, 196.

95   Ibid.

96   Alexander Simpson, *The Life and Travels of Thomas Simpson, The Arctic Discoverer* (Toronto: Baxter Publishing Company, 1963), 136-37.

97   John W. Garvin, ed., *Voyages*, 125n.

98   Richard Glover, ed., *Thompson's Narrative*, 312.

99   Ibid., 313.

100 R.O. Merriman, "The Bison and the Fur Trade," *Queen's Quarterly* vol. 34, 84.

101 Vilhjalmur Stefansson, *The Fat of the Land*, 198.

102 Fort Chipewyan Journal, Alberta Provincial Library, 16 September 1823.

103 Richard Glover, ed., *Thompson's Narrative*, 312.

104 Elliot Coues, ed., *New Light on the early history of the greater Northwest: The manuscript journals of Alexander Henry, fur trader of the Northwest Company, and of David Thompson, official geographer and explorer of the same company, 1799-1814; exploration and adventure among the Indians on the Red, Saskatchewan, Missouri and Columbia Rivers* vol. 2 (New York: F.P. Harper, 1897), 539, 13 September 1809.

105 Edwin E. Rich, ed., *Journal of Occurrences*, 267.

106 J.B. Tyrrell, ed., *Journals*, 452.

107 HBCA/PAM B.39/a/29, Fort Chipewyan Post Journals, 27 April 1834. The Great Slave Lake and Mackenzie River regions lacked the animals necessary to make dry provisions.

108 HBCA/PAM B.39/a/4, Nottingham House Journals, 6 May 1804.

109 Ibid., B.39/a/3, 16 November 1803.

110 HBCA/PAM B.39/e/3, p. 20, Fort Chipewyan Report on District.

111 Ibid.

112 William K. Lamb, ed., *Sixteen Years in Indian Country*, 26.

113 HBCA/PAM B.39/a/4, Nottingham House Journals, 16 September 1804.

114 Fort Chipewyan Journal, Alberta Provincial Library, 15 August 1823.

115 R. King, *Narrative of a Journey*, vol. 1, 82-83.

116 HBCA/PAM B.39/a/15, Fort Chipewyan Post Journals, 1819-20, 3 November 1819.

117 Fort Chipewyan Journal, Alberta Provincial Library, 2 August 1822.

118 Ibid., 30 October 1822.

119 HBCA/PAM B.39/a/29, Fort Chipewyan Post Journals, 1831-34, 19 September 1833.

120 J.B. Tyrrell, ed., *Journals*, 508.

121 Ibid., 452.

122 R. King, *Narrative of a Journey*, vol. 1, 97.

123 See, for example, Edwin E. Rich, ed., *Journal of Occurrences*, 44. Harmon mentions this as well, see William K. Lamb, ed., *Sixteen Years in Indian Country*, 115.

124 HBCA/PAM B.39/a/1, Nottingham House Journals, 21 March 1803.

125 HBCA/PAM B.39/a/29, Fort Chipewyan Post Journals, 1831-34, 16 September 1833.

126 Public Archives of Canada (hereafter PAC). Journal of John Porter, 19 May 1800.

127 HBCA/PAM B.39/e/5, p. 7, Fort Chipewyan Report on District, 1822-23.

128 HBCA/PAM B.39/a/22, Fort Chipewyan Post Journals, 1823-24. Copy of Letters relating to Athabasca, J. Keith to W. McKintosh, dated Fort Chipewyan, 5 December 1823.

129 Ibid.

130 Edwin E. Rich, ed., *Robertson's Correspondence*, cxviii.

131 Fort Chipewyan Journal, Alberta Provincial Library, 27 November 1822, 4 February, 18 March 1823.

132 Ibid., 11 December 1823.

133 Ibid., 4 March 1823.

134 Ibid., 5 September 1823. The construction of a boat took about twenty-five working days.

135 Ibid., 21 May 1823.

136 HBCA/PAM B.29/e/6, p. 13, Fort Chipewyan Report on District, 1823-24.

137 Ibid., p. 14. Keith estimated the average cost per piece for boats at £68 11s. 3d. while for canoes the cost more than doubled.

4. THE FORT AND THE MEN WHO SERVED IT

1 HBCA/PAM B.39/a/1, Nottingham House Journals, 9 May 1803, 15 August 1802; HBCA/PAM B.39/a/3, Nottingham House Journals, 1802-03, 15 August 1802.

2 Arthur S. Morton, *History of the Canadian West*, 508. See also, Edwin E. Rich, *History of the Hudson's Bay Company*, vol. 2, 273-74.

3 HBCA/PAM B.39/a/3, Nottingham House Journals, 1803-04, 18 March 1804.

4 Ibid., 1804-05; HBCA/PAM B.39/a/4, 18 May 1805.

5 A "pork-eater" or *mangeur de larde*, was an *engagé* hired to man the canoes between Montreal and Grand Portage. The *engagé* who went beyond the Grand Portage was known as *un homme du nord*. The Athabasca men, however, considered a true *homme du nord* to be one who had crossed the Portage La Loche.

6 Arthur S. Morton, ed., *The Journal of Duncan McGillivray of the North West Company at Fort George on the Saskatchewan, 1794-1795* (Toronto: The Macmillan Company, 1929), 11.

7 James Alton James, *Scientific Exploration*, 47.

8 George Back, *Narrative*, 39.

9 Richard Glover, ed., *Thompson's Narrative*, 133.

10 John Richardson, *Arctic Searching Expedition, a Journal of a Boat Voyage through Rupert's Land and the Arctic Sea, in Search of the Discovery Ships under Command of Sir John Franklin. With an Appendix on the Physical Geography of North America*, vol.

1 (London: Longman, Brown, Green, and Longmans, 1851), 92, 19 June 1848.

11 George Back, *Narrative*, 66-67.

12 Ibid.

13 J. Richardson, *Arctic Searching Expedition*, vol. 1, 111.

14 Ibid., 11.

15 George Back, *Narrative*, 70.

16 J. Richardson, *Arctic Searching Expedition*, vol. 1, 99.

17 Ibid., 104.

18 J.B. Tyrrell, ed., *Journals*, 446, 14 October 1791.

19 Edwin E. Rich, ed., *Journal of Occurrences*, 49.

20 Ibid.

21 George Back, *Narrative*, 64, 5 July 1833. Mr. Noel Mackay and Mr. Victor Mercredi, late of Fort Chipewyan, recalled this custom was practiced in the early years of the twentieth century when the crews of the scows and sturgeon-heads arrived from Athabasca Landing. There is certainly a desire to appear in one's finest attire after grueling days of paddling, insects, rain, and scorching sun, if only to show that the voyage was performed in a manner worthy of the *hommes du nord*.

22 J.B. Tyrrell, ed., *Journals*, 446, 6 October 1791; HBCA/PAM B.39/a/3, 22 September 1803; Edwin E. Rich, ed., *Journal of Occurrences*, 69, 30 September 1820; Fort Chipewyan Journal, Alberta Provincial Library, 24 September 1823.

23 Ibid.

24 J. Richardson in J. Franklin, *Narrative of a Second Expedition*, 216, March 1820.

25 G. Back in J. Franklin, *Narrative of a Second Expedition*, vol. 2, 68-69.

26 Ibid., vol. 1, 339, 13 August 1820.

27 John W. Garvin, ed., *Voyages*, 95n.

28 HBCA/PAM B.39/e/3, p. 2, Fort Chipewyan Report on District, 1820-21.

29 HBCA/PAM B.39/e/9, p. 8, Fort Chipewyan Report on District, 1825-26.

30 L.R. Masson, *Bourgeois*, vol. 1, 111.

31 G. Stanley, ed., *In Search of the Magnetic North*, 170.

32 HBCA/PAM B.39/a/14, Fort Chipewyan Post Journals, 1818-19.

33 Fort Chipewyan Journal, Alberta Provincial Library, 19 September 1822.

34 G. Stanley, ed., *In Search of the Magnetic North*, 89.

35 Ibid., 93.

36 Fort Chipewyan Journal, Alberta Provincial Library, 26 August 1822.

37 Ibid., 7 June 1823.

38 Ibid., 1 November 1822.

39 HBCA/PAM B.39/a/29, Fort Chipewyan Post Journals, 1 January 1833.

40 HBCA/PAM B.39/a/28, Fort Chipewyan Post Journals, 1 January 1832. Twist tobacco was tobacco leaves twisted into long ropes. It was given out by measurement; six feet of tobacco weighed about ¾ of a pound. Cf. Charles M. Gates, ed., *Five Fur Traders*, 129n.

41 Edwin E. Rich, ed., *Journal of Occurrences*, 88, 20 October 1820.

42 Ibid., 395-96.

43 Ibid. Emphasis by author.

44 John W. Garvin, ed., *Voyages*, 122.

45 Ibid., 122n. Emphasis by author.

46 MUMC. Journal of James Mackenzie, 9 April 1800.

47 "An Account of the Athabasca Indians by a Partner of the North West Company," Manuscript, McGill University Library, 7. G.C. Davidson dates this 1795, in *The North West Company*, 233.

48 MUMC. Journal of James Mackenzie, 18 April 1800. Compare with Turnor's remarks in his journal in J.B. Tyrrell, ed., *Journals*, 446, 28 April 1792.

49 Richard Glover, ed., *Journey*, 67-68.

50 Ibid., 170.

51 HBCA/PAM B.39/a/29, Fort Chipewyan Post Journals, 1831-34, 14 November 1832.

52 R. Fleming, ed., *Minutes of Council Northern Department of Rupert Land, 1821-1831* (London: The Hudson's Bay Record Society, 1940), 60, 5 July 1823, Resolution 153.

53 Fort Chipewyan Journal, Alberta Provincial Library, 30 November 1823.

5. THE INDIANS, FORT CHIPEWYAN, AND THE METHODS OF TRADE

1 Richard Glover, ed., *Journey*, xxix.

2 John W. Garvin, ed., *Voyages*, 119-20.

3 J. Richardson, *Arctic Searching Expedition*, 4-5.

4 Diamond Jenness, "The Indian Background of Canadian History," National Museum of Canada, Bulletin No. 86, p. 36.

5 Arthur S. Morton, *History of the Canadian West*, 12.

6 Ibid., 289.

7 HBCA/PAM B.39/e/8, p. 6, Fort Chipewyan Report on District, 1824-25.

8 For a complete discussion of the barren ground caribou and their migratory habits see C.H.D. Clarke, "A Biological Investigation of the Thelon Game Sanctuary," National Museum of Canada, Bulletin No. 96, pp. 84-112.

9 Richard Glover, ed., *Journey*, 51.

10 Ibid., 212-13.

11 J.B. Tyrrell, ed., *Journals*, 450.

12 Ibid., 450-51.

13 Richard Glover, ed., *Journey*, 24.

14 Ibid., 26.

15 Edwin E. Rich, ed., *Journal of Occurrences*, 355-56.

16 Richard Glover, ed., *Journey*, 51.

17 HBCA/PAM B.39/a/29, Fort Chipewyan Post Journals, 1831-34, 6 October 1833. Guy H. Blanchet made mention of this group in 1926:

> These people seldom visit the posts, but spend the year in the upper plateau, moving out to meet the caribou in the late summer and returning down-stream after the spring break-up to the good fish lakes. . . . The camps of the Caribou Eaters are truly pleasant places, set with an eye to beauty in a beautiful country. Their seasonal drift is through picturesque and excellent waterways by which, if they wish, all parts of the plateau may be reached.

See Guy H. Blanchet, "New Light on Forgotten Trails in the Far Northwest," *The Canadian Field-Naturalist* 40 (April/May 1926): 69-75, 96-99.

18 HBCA/PAM B.39/a/3, Nottingham House Journals, 1803-04, 13 March 1804.

19 HBCA/PAM B.39/e/8, p. 6, Fort Chipewyan Report on District, 1824-25.

20 HBCA/PAM B.39/e/9, p. 8, Fort Chipewyan Report on District, 1825-26.

21 Richard Glover, ed., *Journey*, 69. See also pages 79 and 92.

22 MUMC. Journal of James Mackenzie, 20 April, 10 June, 4 August 1800.

23 *En derouine* was used to encourage the Indians to work industriously at trapping because once they had received their credits, they were less inclined to exert themselves. During competitive times the practice became much more significant.

24 HBCA/PAM B.39/a/1, Nottingham House Journals, 1802-03, 13 October 1802.

25 PAC. Selkirk Papers, MG 19 E 1(1), vol. 30, 9130, John McGillivray to McGillis and Stewart, dated Dunvegan, 15 December 1815.

26 Ibid., 9132.

27 John W. Garvin, ed., *Voyages*, 126.

28 Ibid., 127.

29 Richard Glover, ed., *Journey*, 52. See also Mackenzie's

comment that they were always concerned with "the advancement of their own interests" in John W. Garvin, ed., *Voyages*, 127.

30 Edwin E. Rich, in his seminal article "Trade Habits and Economic Motivation Among the Indians of North America" in *The Canadian Journal of Economics and Political Science* 26, no. 1 (February 1960): 35-53, was the first to discuss this difference.

31 Ibid., 49.

32 MUMC. Journal of James Mackenzie, 17 February 1800.

33 Richard Glover, ed., *Journey*, 186.

34 HBCA/PAM B.39/e/8, p. 30, Fort Chipewyan Report on District, 1824-25.

35 J. Richardson, *Arctic Searching Expedition*, vol. 2, 27.

36 HBCA/PAM B.39/a/15, Fort Chipewyan Post Journals, 1819-20, 31 March 1820.

37 Ibid.

38 Edwin E. Rich, ed., *Journal of Occurrences*, 310, 28 March 1821.

39 MUMC. Journal of James Mackenzie, 2 April 1800.

40 Fort Chipewyan Journal, Alberta Provincial Library, 26 May 1823.

41 HBCA/PAM B.39/a/29, Fort Chipewyan Post Journals, 10 April 1833.

42 HBCA/PAM B.39/e/6, p. 5, Fort Chipewyan Report on District, 1823-24.

43 John W. Garvin, ed., *Voyages*, 127. The flux and consumption were probably bowel disorders and tuberculosis respectively.

44 HBCA/PAM B.39/a/3, Nottingham House Journals, 5 September 1802.

45 Ibid., 30 September 1803.

46 Ibid., 5 September 1803.

47 HBCA/PAM B.39/a/15, Fort Chipewyan Post Journals, 1819-20, 27 October 1819.

48 Ibid., 20 December 1819, 28 January 1820.

49 Ibid. The illness crippled the fur hunts.

50 HBCA/PAM B.39/a/29, Fort Chipewyan Post Journals, 1831-34, 10 April 1833.

51 Richard Glover, ed., *Journey,* 219.

52 PAC. Journal of John Porter, Masson Collection, MG 19 C 1, vol. 6, 28 July 1800.

53 HBCA/PAM B.39/a/15, Fort Chipewyan Post Journals, 1819-20, 16 March 1820.

54 HBCA/PAM B.39/a/29, Fort Chipewyan Post Journals, 1831-34, 9 March 1833.

55 HBCA/PAM B.39/a/3, Nottingham House Journals, 1803-04, 13 September 1803.

56 Edwin E. Rich, ed., *Journal of Occurrences,* 197, 9 December 1820.

57 HBCA/PAM B.39/a/29, Fort Chipewyan Post Journals, 1831-34, 30 April 1833.

58 "Journal of a Journey with the Chepewyans or Northern Indians, to the Slave Lake, & to the East & west of the Slave River, in 1791 & 2, by Peter Fidler," in J.B. Tyrrell, ed., *Journals,* 553.

59 Ibid.

60 John W. Garvin, ed., *Voyages,* 127.

61 J.B. Tyrrell, ed., *Journals,* 452.

62 Ibid., 458.

63 R. Fleming, ed., *Minutes of Council,* 168, 26 June 1826, Resolution 130; PAC. John McLeod Papers, 1811-1837, MG 19 A 23, pp. 172-73, Alexander Stewart to Governor, Chief Factors, and Chief Traders, dated Fort Chipewyan, 28 September 1826; J. Richardson, *Arctic Searching Expedition,* vol. 2, 31.

64 MUMC. Journal of James Mackenzie, 16 August 1799.

65 PAC. Journal of John Porter, 5 October 1800.

66 Ibid.

67 Richard Glover, ed., *Journey,* 198-99.

68 HBCA/PAM B.39/a/3, Nottingham House Journals, 11

October 1803.

69 Ibid., 23 January 1804.

70 HBCA/PAM B.39/a/1, Nottingham House Journals, 1802-03, 4 October 1802.

71 HBCA/PAM B.39/e/3, p. 18, Fort Chipewyan Report on District, 1820-21.

72 Edwin E. Rich, ed., *Journal of Occurrences*, 358.

73 Ibid., 73, 3 October 1820.

74 HBCA/PAM B.39/e/3, p. 22, Fort Chipewyan Report on District, 1820-21.

75 Edwin E. Rich, *Journal of Occurrences*, 73, 3 October 1820.

76 HBCA/PAM B.39/e/5, p. 9, Fort Chipewyan Report on District, 1822-23.

77 HBCA/PAM B.39/e/9, p. 3, Fort Chipewyan Report on District, 1825-26.

78 Ibid., p. 4.

79 Ibid.

80 Ibid.

81 Ibid., p. 7.

82 Edwin E. Rich, ed., *Simpson's 1828 Journey to the Columbia. Part of Dispatch from George Simpson Esqr. Governor of Ruperts Land to the Governor and Committee of the Hudson's Bay Company London* (London: The Hudson's Bay Record Society, 1947), 8-9.

83 HBCA/PAM B.39/a/27, Fort Chipewyan Post Journals, 1828-29, 30 March 1829.

84 W.S. Wallace, ed., *John McLean's Notes of a Twenty-Five Year's Service in the Hudson's Bay Territory* (Toronto: The Champlain Society, 1932), 137.

6. MAKING THE ATHABASCA PAY: THE ECONOMICS OF A DISTRICT DEPOT

1 Harold A. Innis, *The Fur Trade*, 274.

2 L.R. Masson, *Bourgeois,* vol. 1, Wentzell's Letters, to Roderick Mackenzie, 28 February 1814, pp. 110-11.

3 Harold A. Innis, *The Fur Trade,* 199-200.

4 Gordon C. Davidson, *The North West Company,* Appendix J, 280.

5 Ibid.

6 J.B. Tyrrell, ed., *Journals,* 122-23. In 1774 Samuel Hearne noted that the Canadians were paying from £20 to £50 for similar services performed in the interior.

7 E.H. Oliver, ed., *The Canadian Northwest, its early development and legislative records,* vol. 2 (Ottawa: Government Printing Bureau, 1914-15), 749.

8 Harold A. Innis, *The Fur Trade,* 241.

9 W.S. Wallace, *Documents Relating to the North West Company* (Toronto: The Champlain Society, 1934), 272, 287.

10 HBCA/PAM B.39/e/4, p. 8, Fort Chipewyan Report on District, 1821-22.

11 HBCA/PAM B.39/e/5, p. 2, Fort Chipewyan Report on District, 1822-23.

12 Ibid.

13 HBCA/PAM B.39/e/6, p. 3, Fort Chipewyan Report on District, 1823-24. The Chipewyans numbered 243 men, 160 women and 90 girls; the Crees included 16 men, 14 women and 30 children.

14 HBCA/PAM B.39/e/8, p. 5, Fort Chipewyan Report on District, 1824-25.

15 HBCA/PAM B.39/e/9, p. 44, Fort Chipewyan Report on District, 1825-26.

16 Ibid.

17 HBCA/PAM B.39/a/29, Fort Chipewyan Post Journals, 15 October 1834. This figure cannot be taken as anything more than approximate.

18 HBCA/PAM B.39/d/9, pp. 37-45, Fort Chipewyan Account Book, 1821-22.

19 HBCA/PAM B.39/e/4, Fort Chipewyan Report on District,

1821-22.

20 HBCA/PAM B.39/e/6, p. 2, Fort Chipewyan Report on District, 1823-24. There were 57 men, 24 women, and 37 children, including extra people needed for the Land Arctic Expedition of John Franklin.

21 Ibid., p. 3.

22 Ibid., p. 4.

23 Ibid., p. 9

24 HBCA/PAM B.39/e/9, p. 13, Fort Chipewyan Report on District, 1825-26. The Mackenzie River transport became a separate system, meaning a yearly saving of £1,200. See R. Fleming, ed., *Minutes of Council*, xxxvi.

25 HBCA/PAM B.39/e/9, p. 13, Fort Chipewyan Report on District, 1825-26.

26 HBCA/PAM B.39/a/26, p. 6, Fort Chipewyan Post Journals, 1827-28.

27 HBCA/PAM B.39/a/29, 8 October 1832, Fort Chipewyan Post Journals.

28 Arthur S. Morton, *History of the Canadian West*, 353.

29 Duke of Rochefoucault-Liancourt, *Travels Through the United States of North America the Country of the Iroquois and Upper Canada, in the years 1795, 1796 and 1797; with an Authentic Account of Lower Canada* (London: T. Hurst & J. Wallis, 1799), 330.

30 Edwin E. Rich, ed., *Journal of Occurrences*, 72, 2 October 1820. Ibid., 398.

31 See, for example, Arthur S. Morton, *History of the Canadian West*, 354.

32 Duke of Rochefoucault-Liancourt, *Travels*, 331.

33 Gordon C. Davidson, *The North West Company*, 235.

34 Arthur S. Morton, *History of the Canadian West*, 331.

35 HBCA/PAM B.39/d/4a, pp. 28-33, Fort Chipewyan Account Book, 1819-20.

36 HBCA/PAM B.39/d/9, pp. 37-45, Fort Chipewyan Account Book, 1821-22.

37 MUMC. Journal of James Mackenzie, 7 January 1800. In 1820, Simpson, although urged by the Committee to reduce prices, held the opinion that as long as high wages were paid, high prices must be charged. See Edwin E. Rich, ed., *Journal of Occurrences*, 72n.

38 Ibid., 12 January 1800.

39 PAC. Selkirk Papers, MG 19 E 1(1), vol. 30, 9144. John McGillivray to William McGillivray, dated Dunvegan, 17 January 1816.

40 Edwin E. Rich, ed., *Journal of Occurrences*, 398.

41 R. Fleming, ed., *Minutes of Council*, Appendix II, 347, Simpson to Governor and Committee, dated York Factory, 31 July 1822.

42 Ibid., 349.

43 Ibid., 118, 2 July 1825, Resolution 82.

44 HBCA/PAM B.39/a/29, Fort Chipewyan Post Journals, 1 June 1833.

45 HBCA/PAM B.39/e/9, pp. 41-42, Fort Chipewyan Account Book, 1825-26.

46 HBCA/PAM B.39/d/4, pp. 26-27, Fort Chipewyan Account Book, 1830-31. This account lists Norway House and inland advances which provides a more complete picture than the above mentioned 1825-26 account. See Table 11.

47 HBCA/PAM B.39/e/8, p. 5, Fort Chipewyan Report on District, 1824-25.

48 PAC. The North West Papers, MG 19 A 30, vol. 1, C.N. Bell Collection, Alexander Fisher to Donald Ross, dated Great Slave Lake, 21 September 1841.

49 See, for example, Harold A. Innis, *The Fur Trade*, 241.

50 PAC. Selkirk Papers, MG 19 E 1(1), vol. 30, 9144, John McGillivray to William McGillivray.

51 Edwin E. Rich, ed., *Robertson's Correspondence*, 81, No. 22, C. Robertson to G. Moffat, dated Fort Chipewyan, February 1819.

52 See Table 2.

53 A first class clerk was one who had at least three years' experience as a clerk.

54 R. Fleming, ed., *Minutes of Council,* Appendix A, 305, The Governor and Committee to Simpson, London, 27 February 1822.

55 Ibid., 346, Simpson to the Governor and Committee, York Factory, 31 July 1822.

56 Ibid., 346.

57 L.R. Masson, *Bourgeois,* vol. 1, 150, Wentzell's Letters, dated Mackenzie's River, 1 March 1824.

58 R. Fleming, ed., *Minutes of Council,* Appendix A, 357-58. Cf., Edwin E. Rich, ed., *Robertson's Correspondence,* 119.

59 For discussions of the circumstances surrounding the amalgamation, see Arthur S. Morton, *History of the Canadian West,* 613-14; Edwin E. Rich, *History of the Hudson's Bay Company,* 385 ff.; and Edwin E. Rich, ed., *Robertson's Correspondence,* xcix.

60 As quoted in Gordon C. Davidson, *The North West Company,* 234.

61 L.R. Masson, *Bourgeois,* vol. 1, 44, Reminiscences of R. Mackenzie, A. Mackenzie to R. Mackenzie dated Fort Chipewyan, 13 January 1794. The remarks also give a hint to the ambitious character of Alexander Mackenzie.

62 L.R. Masson, *Bourgeois,* vol. 1, 93. Wentzell's name was apparently spelled in two ways. See Edwin E. Rich, ed., *Journal of Occurrences,* 472, and L.R. Masson, *Bourgeois,* vol. 1, 67.

63 Ibid., 94.

64 Harold A. Innis, *The Fur Trade,* 248.

65 L.R. Masson, *Bourgeois,* vol. 1, Wentzell's Letters.

66 Edwin E. Rich, ed., *History of the Hudson's Bay Company,* vol. 1, 436, vol. 2, 115. See also Arthur S. Morton, *History of the Canadian West,* 289, 296, 299.

67 Richard Glover, ed., *Journey,* 115. The term "made beaver" meant one full-grown beaver skin. This was the standard against which all other skins were rated. This system is well

explained in Richard Glover, ed., *Journey*, 114-15.

68 Ibid., 116n.

69 PAC. North West Company, Letter Book, 1798-1802, MG 19 B1. Alexander Mackenzie to Messrs. McTavish, Frobisher and Co., dated Mackinack, 4 June 1799.

70 J.B. Tyrrell, ed., *Journals*, 457.

71 Harold A. Innis, *The Fur Trade*, 229.

72 W.S. Wallace, *Documents*, Minutes of the North West Company, 260-61, 264-65.

73 Quoted in Edwin E. Rich, ed., *Robertson's Correspondence*, xxvi, 10 January 1810.

74 Harold A. Innis, *The Fur Trade*, 258.

75 Edwin E. Rich, ed., *Journal of Occurrences*, 363.

76 HBCA/PAM B.39/e/3, p. 20, Fort Chipewyan Report on District, 1820-21 .

77 Edwin E. Rich, ed., *Journal of Occurrences*, 364.

78 PAC. Selkirk Papers, MG 19 E 1(1), vol. 30, 9114-9116. Simon McGillivray to McTavish, McGillivrays & Company, dated London, 1 June 1811.

79 Ibid. , vol. 29, 8794.   George Keith to Thomas Thain, dated Fort William, 26 July 1816. Keith is discussing the Athabasca district.

80 Ibid. See also HBCA/PAM F.3/2, p. 170, North West Company Correspondence, 1800-27. Simon McGillivray (Junior) to Angus Shaw, dated Fort Chipewyan, 15 November 1818.

81 PAC. Selkirk Papers, MG 19 E 1(1), vol. 28, 8697. John Stuart to James Grant, dated Lac la Pluie, 7 August 1816.

82 L.R. Masson, *Bourgeois*, vol. 1, 120, Wentzell's Letters, dated Lac la Pluie, 4 August 1818.

83 HBCA/PAM B.39/e/3, p. 24, Fort Chipewyan Report on District.

84 The 1814-15 expedition cost the Hudson's Bay Company well over £10,000. Edwin E. Rich, ed., *Robertson's Correspondence*, lxxiv; Ibid., lxxxiv.

85 HBCA/PAM F.3/2, p. 168, North West Company

Correspondence, 1800-27. Simon McGillivray (Junior) to Angus Shaw, dated Fort Chipewyan, 4 October 1818.

86 Ibid. Robert Miles's notes confirm this event in HBCA/PAM B.39/a/14, Fort Chipewyan Post Journals, 3 October 1818.

87 HBCA/PAM F.3/2, p. 176, North West Company Correspondence, 1800-27. J.G. McTavish to North West Proprietors, dated Peace River, 13 December 1818.

88 Ibid., p. 177.

89 HBCA/PAM B.39/a/15, Fort Chipewyan Post Journals, 6 October 1819.

90 Ibid., 27 October, 20 December 1819, 18 January, 27 January, 2 February, 16 March 1820. Also HBCA/PAM B.39/e/3, p. 20, Fort Chipewyan Report on District. According to Wentzell, these sicknesses made their appearance with German settlers in 1819 at Selkirk's Red River colony. He said that one-fifth of the Indian population died as a result. L.R. Masson, *Bourgeois*, vol. 1, Wentzell's Letters, 130, dated Great Slave Lake, 23 May 1820; HBCA/PAM B.39/e/3, p. 20, Fort Chipewyan Report on District, 1820-21.

91 Edwin E. Rich, ed., *Robertson's Correspondence*, 269, 272. For a brief biography see Edwin E. Rich, ed., *Journal of Occurrences*, Appendix B, 471-72.

92 Quoted in Edwin E. Rich, ed., *Robertson's Correspondence*, xxvi. Emphasis by author.

93 Ibid., xciv.

94 Edwin E. Rich, ed., *Journal of Occurrences*, 358.

95 Ibid., 355-56.

96 R. Fleming, ed., *Minutes of Council*, Appendix II, 338, G. Simpson to Governor and Committee, dated York Factory, 16 July 1822.

97 HBCA/PAM B.39/e/4, p. 7, Fort Chipewyan Report on District, 1821-22.

98 Ibid. See above for discussion of the problem of reducing the number of employees.

99 The freemen and Iroquois rapidly depleted fur fields by

indiscriminate killing of animals, young and old, in all seasons. Their role in the fur trade requires further study. See also Arthur S. Morton, *History of the Canadian West*, 355, and Edwin E. Rich, ed., *Journal of Occurrences*, 384.

100 HBCA/PAM B.39/e/4, p. 8, Fort Chipewyan Report on District, 1821-22.

101 Ibid.

102 Ibid., p. 7.

103 HBCA/PAM B.39/a/22, Fort Chipewyan Post Journals, 1823-24. Copy of Letters relating to Athabasca, James Keith and Peter Dease to Governor, Chief Factors, and Chief Traders, dated Fort Chipewyan, 5 December 1823.

104 HBCA/PAM B.39/e/6, p. 6, Fort Chipewyan Report on District, 1823-24.

105 Ibid.

106 Ibid.

107 Ibid.

108 HBCA/PAM B.39/e/9, p. 6, Fort Chipewyan Report on District, 1825-26.

109 HBCA/PAM B.39/e/8, p. 21, Fort Chipewyan Report on District, 1824-25.

110 Ibid., pp. 2-3.

111 HBCA/PAM B.39/e/9, p. 6, Fort Chipewyan Report on District, 1825-26.

112 Ibid.

113 Ibid., p. 43.

114 HBCA/PAM B.39/e/8, p. 11, Fort Chipewyan Report on District, 1824-25. The late arrivals of brigades was occasioned by the recent introduction of boats and the experimentation with a different route. See Edwin E. Rich, ed., *Journal of Occurrences*, xxxvi, ff.

115 HBCA/PAM B.39/e/9, p. 18, Fort Chipewyan Report on District, 1825-26.

116 Ibid.

117 R. Fleming, ed., *Minutes of Council*, lxi.

118 Edwin E. Rich, *History of the Hudson's Bay Company*, vol. 2, 475. For a brief biographical sketch see Edwin E. Rich, ed., *Journal of Occurrences*, Appendix B, 444.

CONCLUSION

1 HBCA/PAM B.39/e/3, p. 8, Fort Chipewyan Report on District, 1820-21.

2 The fur of a South American rodent.

3 H.T. Martin, *Castorologia; or The history and traditions of the Canadian beaver* (Montreal: Drysdale, 1892), 47; Harold A. Innis, *The Fur Trade*, 334-35.

4 Edwin E. Rich, ed., *Robertson's Correspondence*, xxxviii, lxxvii.

5 Ibid., 36.

6 For example, the location of the fort.

7 Its financial position was weak; the War of 1812 had cut off markets and sources of supply, and dissension was growing between the agents and wintering partners. See Edwin E. Rich, ed., *Robertson's Correspondence*, lx-lxi.

APPENDIX

1 For an excellent account of the value of furs and packs see W. Baergen, "The Fur Trade At Lesser Slave Lake, 1815-1831" (M.A. thesis, University of Alberta, 1967). It is necessary to point out, however, that beaver is sold by weight and not by pelt, as Mr. Baergen states.

2 MUMC. Journal of James Mackenzie, 8 April 1800.

3 I am indebted to Mr. Paul Kelpin, former Hudson's Bay Company manager at Fort Chipewyan, for the information on the weight of beaver.

4 Arthur S. Morton, *History of the Canadian West*, 355.

5 Ibid.

6 Edwin E. Rich, ed., *Robertson's Correspondence*, 89n.

7 HBCA/PAM B.39/e/9, p. 42, Fort Chipewyan Report on District, 1825-26.

8 Harold A. Innis, *The Fur Trade*, 318.

9 Ibid., 240n.

10 Elliot Coues, *New Light*, vol. 1, 283.

11 Gordon C. Davidson, *The North West Company*, 206n.

12 HBCA/PAM B.39/e/9, p. 42, Fort Chipewyan Report on District, 1825-26.

13 Ibid.

14 Frederick Merk, *Fur Trade and Empire* (Cambridge: Harvard University Press, 1931), 70.

15 Edwin E. Rich, ed., *Simpson's 1828 Journey*, 24-25.

16 Ibid.

17 HBCA/PAM B.39/e/6, p. 15, Fort Chipewyan Report on District, 1823-24.

18 HBCA/PAM B.39/e/8, p. 5, Fort Chipewyan Report on District, 1824-25.

SELECT BIBLIOGRAPHY

MANUSCRIPT SOURCES

1. *Alberta Provincial Library.*
   Fort Chipewyan Journal, 1822-24.

2. *Hudson's Bay Company Archives, Provincial Archives of Manitoba* (Microfilm).
   Nottingham House Journals, 1802-06.
   Fort Chipewyan Post Journals, 1815-34.
   Fort Chipewyan Reports on District, 1820-26.
   Fort Chipewyan Account Books, 1817-35.
   Fort Chipewyan Correspondence Book, 1818-35.
   North West Company Papers.

3. *Public Archives of Canada.*
   Selkirk Correspondence.
   North West Papers.
   Masson Collection.

4. *McGill University.*
   Masson Collection.

PUBLISHED SOURCES

Back, George. *Narrative of the Arctic Land Expedition to the Mouth of the Great Fish River, and Along the Shores of the Arctic Ocean, in the Years 1833, 1834, and 1835.* London: John Murray, 1836.

Barbeau, Marius. "The House That Mac Built." *The Beaver* (December 1945).

Blanchet, Guy. "Emporium of the North." *The Beaver* (March 1946).

Bryce, George. *The Remarkable History of the Hudson's Bay Company.* London: Sampson, Low, Marston, 1910.

Burpee, Lawrence J. *The Search for the Western Sea.* Toronto: Musson Book Company, 1908.

Cameron, Agnes D. *The New North; Being Some Account of a Woman's Journey through Canada to the Arctic*. New York: D. Appleton & Co., 1912.

Clarke, C.H.D. "A Biological Investigation of the Thelon Game Sanctuary." *Bulletin No. 96*, National Museum of Canada (1940): 84-112.

Coues, Elliott, ed. *New Light on the early history of the greater Northwest: The manuscript journals of Alexander Henry, fur trader of the Northwest Company, and of David Thompson, official geographer and explorer of the same company, 1799-1814; exploration and adventure among the Indians on the Red, Saskatchewan, Missouri and Columbia Rivers*. 3 vols. New York: Francis P. Harper, 1897.

Cowie, Isaac. *The Company of Adventurers*. Toronto: William Briggs, 1913.

Davidson, Gordon C. *The North West Company*. Berkeley: University of California Press, 1918.

Dawson, C.A. *The Settlement of the Peace River Country*. Vol. 6 of *Canadian Frontiers of Settlement*. Edited by W.A. Mackintosh and W.L.G. Joerg. Toronto: Macmillan Company of Canada, 1934.

Duchaussois, Reverend Pierre. *Mid Snow and Ice. The Apostles of the North-West*. Ottawa: University of Ottawa, 1937.

_____. *Hidden Apostles, Our Lay Brother Missionaries*. Ottawa: University of Ottawa, 1937.

Fleming, R. Harvey, ed. *Minutes of Council Northern Department of Rupert Land 1821-1831*. Toronto: Champlain Society, 1940.

Franklin, John. *Narrative of a Journey to the Shores of the Polar Sea, in the years 1819, 1820, 1821, and 1822. With an Appendix on Various Subjects Relating to Science and Natural History*. London: J. Murray, 1823.

_____. *Narrative of a Second Expedition to the Shores of the Polar Sea, in the years 1825, 1826, and 1827 Including an*

Account of the Progress of a Detachment to the Eastward, by John Richardson. London: J. Murray, 1828.

Garrioch, Reverend Alfred C. *The Far and Furry North: A Story of Life and Love and Travel in the Days of the Hudson's Bay Company.* Winnipeg: Douglass-McIntyre, 1925.

Garvin, John, ed. *Voyages from Montreal on the River St. Lawrence through the Continent of North America to the Frozen and Pacific Oceans in the years 1789 and 1793 with a Preliminary Account of the Rise, Progress, and Present State of the Fur Trade of that Country by Alexander Mackenzie.* Vol. 3 of *Master-Works of Canadian Authors.* Toronto: The Radisson Society of Canada Limited, 1927. [Original edition published in 1801.]

Gates, Charles M. *Five Fur Traders of the Northwest, being the narrative of Peter Pond and the diaries of John Macdonnell, Archibald N. McLeod, Hugh Faries and Thomas Connor.* St. Paul: Minnesota Historical Society, 1965.

Giraud, Marcel. *Le Métis Canadien, Son Rôle dans l'histoire des Provinces de l'Ouest.* Paris: Institut d'ethnologie, 1945.

Glover, Richard, ed. *David Thompson's Narrative.* Toronto: The Champlain Society, 1962.

Glover, Richard. "The Difficulties of the Hudson's Bay Company's Penetration of the West." *Canadian Historical Review* 29 (September 1948): 250-54.

_____, ed. *A Journey from Prince of Wales's Fort in Hudson's Bay to the Northern Ocean, 1769, 1770, 1771, 1772. By Samuel Hearne.* Toronto: Macmillan Company of Canada Limited, 1958.

Godsell, Philip H. *Arctic Trader: The Account of Twenty Years with the Hudson's Bay Company.* New York: G.P. Putnam's Sons, 1934.

Hunter, Martin. *Canadian Wilds: Tells About the Hudson's Bay Company, Northern Indians and Their Modes of Hunting, Trapping, etc..* Columbus, Ohio: A.R. Harding Publishing Company, 1907.

Innis, Harold A. *The Fur Trade in Canada*. Toronto: University of Toronto Press, 1962. [Original edition published in 1930 by Yale University Press.]

_____. *The Fur Trade of Canada*. Toronto: University of Toronto Library, 1927.

_____. "The North West Company." *Canadian Historical Review* 8 (December 1927): 308-21.

_____. *Peter Pond, Fur Trader and Adventurer*. Toronto: Irwin & Gordon, 1930.

Jenness, Diamond. "The Indian Background of Canadian History." *Bulletin No. 86*. Ottawa: National Museum of Canada (1948).

_____. "The Indians of Canada." *Bulletin No. 65*. Anthropological Series No. 15. Ottawa: National Museum of Canada (1958).

Kemp, H.S.M. *Northern Trader*. Toronto: The Ryerson Press, 1956.

Kennicott, Robert. "The Journal of Robert Kennicott, May 19, 1859 - February 11, 1862." In *The First Scientific Exploration of Russian America and the Purchase of Alaska*, edited by James A. James. Chicago: Northwestern University, 1942.

King, Richard. *Narrative of a Journey to the Shores of the Arctic Ocean, in 1833, 1834, and 1835, under the Command of Captain Back, R.N.*. London: R. Bentley, 1836.

Lamb, W. Kaye, ed. *Sixteen Years in the Indian Country, The Journal of Daniel Williams Harmon, 1800-1816*. Toronto: Macmillan Company of Canada Limited, 1957.

MacGregor, James G. *Peter Fidler: Canada's Forgotten Surveyor 1769-1822*. Toronto: McClelland and Stewart, Ltd., 1966.

MacKay, Douglas. *The Honourable Company*. London: Cassell and Company, Ltd., 1937.

Mair, Charles and Roderick MacFarlane. *Through the Mackenzie Basin: A Narrative of the Athabasca and Peace River*

Treaty Expedition of 1899. Toronto: William Briggs, 1908.

Martin, H.T. *Castorologia; or The history and traditions of the Canadian beaver.* Montreal: Drysdale, 1892.

Masson, L.F.R. *Les Bourgeois de la Compagnie du Nord-Ouest.* Quebec: De l'Imprimerie Générale A. Côté et Cie., 2 vols., 1889.

McKenzie, N.M.W.J. *The Men of the Hudson's Bay Company, 1670 A.D.-1920 A.D., by N.M.W.J. McKenzie.* Fort William, Ontario: Times-Journal Presses, 1921.

Merk, Frederick, *Fur Trade and Empire.* Cambridge: Harvard University Press, 1931.

Moberly, Henry J. *When Fur Was King.* London: J.M. Dent and Sons, Ltd., 1929.

Nute, Grace L. *The Voyageurs Highway.* St. Paul: Minnesota Historical Society, 1941.

Oliver, Edmund H., ed. *The Canadian North-West: Early Development and Legislative Records.* Ottawa: Government Printing Bureau, 2 vols., 1914.

Pike, Warburton. *The Barren Ground of Northern Canada.* London: Macmillan and Company, 1892.

Public Archives of Canada. "Sketch of the Fur Trade of Canada, 1809." 1928, pp. 56-73.

Rich, Edwin E., ed. *Colin Robertson's Correspondence book, September 1817 to September 1822.* Toronto: The Champlain Society, 1939.

_____, ed. *Cumberland House Journals and Inland Journals, 1775-1782. Second Series, 1779-1782.* London: The Hudson's Bay Record Society, 1952.

_____. *Hudson's Bay Company.* London: The Hudson's Bay Record Society, 2 vols., 1959.

_____, ed. *Journal of Occurrences in the Athabasca Department by George Simpson, 1820 and 1821, and Report.* London: The Hudson's Bay Record Society, 1938.

_____, ed. *Simpson's 1828 Journey to the Columbia. Part of Dispatch from George Simpson Esqr. Governor of Ruperts Land to the Governor and Committee of the Hudson's Bay Company London.* London: The Hudson's Bay Record Society, 1947.

_____. "Trade Habits and Economic Motivation Among the Indians of North America." *Canadian Journal of Economics and Political Science* 26 (February 1960): 35-53.

Richardson, John. *Arctic Searching Expedition, a Journal of a Boat Voyage through Rupert's Land and the Arctic Sea, in Search of the Discovery Ships under Command of Sir John Franklin. With an Appendix on the Physical Geography of North America.* London: Longman, Brown, Green, and Longmans, 2 vols., 1851.

Soper, J. Dewey. "History, Range and Home Life of the Northern Bison." *Ecological Monographs* 2 (October 1941): 347-412.

Tyrrell, Joseph B. "Peter Fidler, Trader and Surveyor, 1769-1822." *Proceedings and Transactions of the Royal Society of Canada* 3rd ser., vol. 7, sec. 11 (1913): 117-27.

The Literature of Fur Trade History Since 1967

Patricia A. Myers

The writing of Canadian history has achieved a long and varied tradition parallel to the history it strives to interpret.[1] The recent past has seen great strides made in both the breadth and depth of Canadian historical scholarship. Turning from a preoccupation with national and political history, a new generation of researchers has brought fresh perspectives encompassing, for example, ethnic, feminist, or labour viewpoints. One of the real beneficiaries of this expanded and sensitive approach has been fur trade studies. When J.M. Parker completed the original edition of his study of early Fort Chipewyan in 1967, "The Fur Trade of Fort Chipewyan on Lake Athabasca, 1778-1835" was one of the first attempts to clarify the nature and activities of a major northwestern fur trade post. His emphasis on social and regional concerns was indicative of the new approach being taken in fur trade studies.

This essay serves only as a guide to some of the more significant literature on the fur trade in the western interior that post-dated the completion of Parker's study. It identifies major developments in interpretation, and points out areas of contention between scholars. In many instances, the bibliographies and footnotes cited will lead the interested reader to more detailed or specific studies. The advances in interpretation have been both assisted and enhanced by the voluminous increase in factual detail available, whether it be of structural components or material culture. Current scholars can draw on a rich body of published literature not available to their predecessors.

Several works make general overviews of the fur trade easily accessible for the interested reader. E.E. Rich's *The Fur Trade and the Northwest to 1857* just post-dated the completion of Parker's study. Daniel Francis provides a lively chronological summary in *Battle for the West: Fur Traders and the Birth of Western Canada.* Relevant chapters of Gerald Friesen's *The Canadian Prairies: A History* are also useful. Glyndwr Williams summarized two hundred years of Hudson's Bay Company history in "The Hudson's Bay Company and the Fur Trade: 1670-1870." Peter C. Newman's popular account, *The Company of Adventurers*, while fast-paced and exciting, sometimes sacrifices accuracy to maintain its compelling narrative.[2]

While past studies focussed on the fur trade from the traders' or companies' perspectives, more recent scholarship has turned its attention to Indian participation in the trade. E.E. Rich first suggested Indian participation may not have been motivated by economics alone and argued that it embodied significant political and social components as well. Abraham Rotstein's was the most persuasive voice advancing this "substantivist" position in the 1970s. He contended the trading ceremonies demanded by the Indians were not simply examples of native ritual, but collective, political actions where alliances and kinship ties were cemented.[3]

Calvin Martin's *Keepers of the Game: Indian-Animal Relationships and the Fur Trade* proved to be the most contentious contribution to the substantivist literature. According to Martin, spiritual beliefs and not economic considerations determined Indian hunters' actions. Indians participated in the fur trade because they had unleashed a war of extermination against fur-bearing animals whose spirits, the Indians believed, were responsible for the devastating epidemic diseases that had swept across North America since the arrival of Europeans. While innovative and challenging, Martin's work suffers from a lack of plausible evidence, and has been harshly criticized. *Indians, Animals and the Fur Trade: A Critique of Keepers of the Game,* a volume of essays edited by Shepard Krech III, marshals this criticism. Krech argued that Martin failed to prove that the Indians commonly believed animal spirits punished humans with diseases, or that the native way to deal with them was to

186

punish rather than appease. Adrian Tanner has been more successful in bringing Indian spiritual beliefs to bear on the fur trade in his examination of how the Crees managed their fur resources.[4]

These interpretations of the nature of the trading process and the Indian motivation to hunt did not go unchallenged. In a series of articles and books, Arthur J. Ray advanced the argument for economic centrality in explaining Indian participation in the fur trade. For Ray, the main factor governing Indian fur trade activity was economics, meaning that the Indian modified his actions according to the available economic opportunities. In this respect, Ray argued, market conditions and not socio-political considerations regulated native actions, and concluded that classical economic theory still provides the best way to determine Indian trade behaviour. In *"Give Us Good Measure": An Economic Analysis of Relations Between the Indians and the Hudson's Bay Company before 1763*, Ray collaborated with Donald Freeman to demonstrate that the Europeans merely used the native trading ceremonies in pursuit of their own economic goals. Through a thorough examination of the traders' system of private profits called "overplus," Ray and Freeman were able to measure the Indians' response to such changing economic conditions as competition between traders.[5]

While these approaches differ fundamentally over the nature of Indian participation in the fur trade, they do share several characteristics representative of the shift evident in fur trade studies. All are concerned with the Indians' role in the trade. All want to determine how and when the fur trade affected Indian societies and economies, and all acknowledge that the fur trade and its effects differed greatly over time and space. This recognition of Indian centrality in the trading process meant aspects of Indian culture joined their white counterparts as important components in the fur trade scenario. Philip Curtain discusses the implications of cross-cultural trade, including the fur trade, in his recent *Cross-Cultural Trade in World History*.[6]

While some Indian cultural traditions changed over time and

space in response to the trade, many others persisted through the fur trade period. The rate of cultural change, and the subsequent decline in native independence, has also sparked debate in the literature. Charles A. Bishop argues that by the early 1700s, the Indians of western James Bay had become dependent on trading posts causing rapid cultural change. Toby Morantz, however, claims there were few significant cultural changes among the inland James Bay Crees by the early 1700s, giving evidence for the persistence of pre-contact society. Morantz's approach is particularly interesting because of the methodology used: she drew detailed "hunter profiles" of the Cree hunters named in the Hudson's Bay Company record books. Using these profiles, she concluded that contact with white traders caused only gradual cultural change, and that even this varied between tribe and location. Agreeing with Robin Fisher's assessment of Indian-white contact in British Columbia, Morantz suggested that significant cultural change did not occur until the era of white settlement.[7]

The recognition of Indian centrality in the fur trade has led to important contributions in the field by ethnohistorians. As Calvin Martin has argued, ethnohistory offers the opportunity to unite the fruits of anthropological research with historical evidence.[8] Of particular interest to Parker's study is the recent work on the northern Athapaskans. James W. Van Stone's *Athapaskan Adaptations: Hunters and Fishermen of the Subarctic Forest* provides a general overview of the ethnography of all Athapaskan tribes.[9] A volume of articles edited by Shepard Krech III includes papers read at the American Society for Ethnohistory conference held in 1981. On the northern Athapaskans, Krech examined trade at Fort Simpson in the early nineteenth century, and concluded that the fur trade demanded demographic, economic and territorial adjustments from the Indians who traded there. Krech further determined, as Carol Judd had for the eastern subarctic, that these adaptions differed not only from tribe to tribe, but from family to family as well. Arthur Ray's contribution upholds his reputation as one of the leaders in the field. He challenged the notion that Indian welfare society is of modern parentage, and traced its origin instead to fur trade conditions.

A new book by J.C. Yerbury shares Ray's conclusions. In *The Subarctic Indians and the Fur Trade 1680-1860*, Yerbury argued that significant changes in the Athapaskan cultural milieu and social organization date from the early fur trade era, and are not products of more modern pressures and conditions. Other scholars disagree. June Helm, E. Rogers and J.G.E. Smith have argued that cultural change in the early contact period was limited, and that only in the post-World War II world has change been substantial. Shepard Krech III has compiled a substantial bibliography listing works in history and anthropology that deal with native Canadians.[10]

One unmistakable result of the contact between native and trader was the progeny of the wilderness unions of white men with native women. The first probings of the nature of the "fur trade society" that emerged form an important part of recent fur trade scholarship. Jennifer H. Brown and Sylvia Van Kirk led the way with important work on family formation in the western interior. In *Strangers in Blood: Fur Trade Company Families in Indian Country,* the anthropologist Brown examined the personnel structures of the Hudson's Bay Company and the North West Company.[11] She discovered that the different cultural backgrounds of the employees recruited by each company created distinct problems both in family formation and for the children of the unions. These problems became particularly acute after the 1821 merger of the two companies.

Sylvia Van Kirk made the first attempt to delineate the role of women in the fur trade in her pathbreaking *"Many Tender Ties": Women in Fur Trade Society, 1670-1870.* Van Kirk argued that fur trade marriages were characterized by affection and stability, and that native women were valued for their wilderness skills and as interpreters and intermediaries in the trade. This nascent system of kinship ties and community formation marked the first stage in the emergence of a distinctive fur trade society. Brown and Van Kirk's analysis of the social history of the fur trade also suggests a new chronology for the contact period based on the eras when native women, then mixed-blood, and finally white women were the preferred mates of fur traders. Van Kirk argues that with the arrival of white women in fur trade society, native and mixed-blood women became the victims of racist attitudes and were relegated to positions of inferiority. In his recent article, "The Fur Trade and the Status of Women in the Western Subarctic," Richard Perry addressed the status of Indian women in a particular native society. He concluded that the harsh treatment meted out to native women by native men during the early contact period was limited in duration and time, and clearly predated the arrival of white women. The low status and harsh treatment accorded women "could be viewed as the result of a cultural system shifting to accommodate a new set of circumstances, with certain aspects exaggerated in the process to the point of stress." Finally, Jennifer Brown's article, "Children of the Early Fur Traders," provides a good overview of an important topic.[12]

The extension of the term Métis to include all people of mixed native/white descent and not just those of native/French descent connected with Red River marks another significant departure in fur trade studies. The most recent research is summarized in a collection of articles edited by Jacqueline Peterson and Jennifer H. Brown entitled *The New Peoples: Being and Becoming Métis in North America*. Most of the contributors presented aspects of their research at the first international conference on the Métis in North America, and the book spans the range of Métis scholarship from community formation and variation to the development of an ethnic consciousness and the resultant problems of identity. The introductory essay by Peterson and Brown attempts to dispel some of the confusion surrounding the use of the term.[13]

Other important contributions to the field of Métis scholarship cannot be overlooked, however. All place the emergence of Métis identity in the context of their participation and role in the fur trade. John Foster provided the first significant discussion of Métis genesis in his article, "The Métis: The People and the Term." Jennifer Brown added another dimension in her article, "Women as Centre and Symbol in the Emergence of Métis Communities." Jacqueline Peterson placed the emergence of Métis identity in their long history of community formation in the Great Lakes region, while Olive Dickason countered that only in the west were those of mixed race free to consider themselves distinctive. Carol Judd and others have argued those of mixed parentage did not always want to be seen as ethnically distinct: some chose to identify with the race of one of their parents. Sylvia Van Kirk's " 'What if Mama is an Indian?': The Cultural Ambivalence of the Alexander Ross Family," most recently available in the Peterson and Brown anthology, thoughtfully explores this problem.[14]

The depth and variety evident in Métis studies reflects the diversity of recent fur trade scholarship as a whole. Numerous ethnic and cultural variations are subsumed in the term Métis; similarly, it is becoming clear that the generalization "the fur trade" is overly simple. There were many fur trades operating in different times and places.[15] The published papers of fur trade conferences indicate the growing range of scholarship. *Old Trails and New Directions: Papers of the Third North American Fur Trade Conference* offers a representative sampling of research on topics including Pacific coast communities, Indian mapping, Orkneymen in the Hudson's Bay Company, and the life of Angus Bethune. The collected papers from the fourth fur trade conference demonstrate an equally broad range of enquiry.

Other areas of fur trade history have also received attention. D.W. Moodie looked at agriculture in the fur trade in a paper presented at the fourth North American fur trade conference, and with Barry Kaye recently co-authored a paper dealing with Indian agriculture in the fur trade.[16] Philip Goldring examined employment in the fur trade in a paper presented at the 1981 meeting of the Canadian Historical Association.

In a more recent paper, he looked at recruitment and advancement in the Hudson's Bay Company between 1834 and 1870. A.A. Den Otter studied the impact of new transportation technology on the Hudson's Bay Company's operations in the northwest between 1857 and 1885. Eric Morse focussed on a different aspect of fur trade transportation history in *Fur Trade Canoe Routes of Canada/Then and Now*. Two biographies are also important: John S. Galbraith's *The Little Emperor: George Simpson and the Hudson's Bay Company* and Marjorie Wilkins Campbell's *Northwest to the Sea: A Biography of William McGillivray*.[17] Adrian Tanner recently lamented the fractured nature of fur trade scholarship in his provocatively titled article, "The End of Fur Trade History." He acknowledged the strengths of the multi-disciplinary approach but decried its inability to produce a theoretical narrative representative of the fur trade experience. Perhaps the new challenge for fur trade studies will be to weave its various components into an appropriate synthesis.

Additional literature on specific topics complements Parker's study of Fort Chipewyan. Charles Bishop and A.J. Ray outlined the pitfalls of ethnohistorical work in "Ethnohistorical Research in the Central Subarctic: Some Conceptual and Methodological Problems." R.P. Janes offered observations on the Mackenzie River Athapaskans from archaeological and ethnohistorical viewpoints. From his examination of the trade in the Athabasca and Mackenzie basins between 1740 and 1814, W.A. Sloan has concluded the declining fur returns in the two areas can be attributed to the gradual withdrawal of the Indians from the trade occasioned by the brutality of the North West Company men. James G.E. Smith, a prolific contributor to the field, has traced Chipewyan, Cree and Inuit relations from 1714 to 1955. Robert Wuetherick's *A History of Fort Chipewyan and the Peace-Athabasca Delta Region* provides a survey of the region from an historical and ecological standpoint. Eric Krause has looked at fur trade fisheries in "The Fisheries of the Hudson's Bay Company at Fort Chipewyan, 1791-1871." Patricia

McCormack brought the study of Fort Chipewyan into the twentieth century with "How the (North) West was Won: Development and Underdevelopment in the Fort Chipewyan Region."[18]

Finally, the recent proliferation of studies dealing with the fur trade's material culture has produced new information on such matters as trade goods, and the structure and layout of forts. Only a few of the many available works contributing to a greater understanding of daily life during the fur trade are mentioned here.

Karlis Karklin's excavations of Nottingham House provided important information about the Athabasca region between 1802 and 1806.[19] His work is complemented by Robert S. Allen's study of Peter Fidler's role at Nottingham House during the same period. Donald Steer's work on fort sites on Methy Portage yielded insights into the role of these significant transfer points. Other works such as those by Robert S. Kidd and Norman and Anne Barka addressed fur trade life at specific forts. Further studies on trade beads, an exhibition catalogue on trade silver, and manuscripts on such topics as trade axes begin to fill in the picture of material culture during the fur trade era.[20]

Recent scholarship has illuminated the context of Fort Chipewyan's history through examinations of cultural changes emerging from native/white contact, family formation, and the various economic components of the fur trade. Our knowledge of the associated material and cultural history is much richer for this enquiry. Research in the historical dimension by geographers, anthropologists, archaeologists, and others has brought fresh and varied perspectives to bear on our understanding of fur trade society. As a result, native Canadian participation in the trade has been recognized and given the centrality it deserves. Future researchers have a firm foundation on which to set the histories of other individual posts like Fort Chipewyan.

NOTES

THE LITERATURE OF FUR TRADE HISTORY
SINCE 1967

1   See, for example, Carl Berger, *The Writing of Canadian History*,
    2nd ed. (Toronto: Oxford University Press, 1986); Margaret
    Conrad, "The Re-birth of Canada's Past: A Decade of
    Women's History," *Acadiensis* (1982): 140-62; J.M. Parker, "The
    Fur Trade of Fort Chipewyan on Lake Athabasca, 1778-1835"
    (unpublished M.A. thesis, University of Alberta, 1967).

2   Edwin E. Rich, *The Fur Trade and the Northwest to 1857*
    (Toronto: McClelland and Stewart, 1967); Daniel Francis,
    Battle for the West: Fur Traders and the Birth of Western Canada
    (Edmonton: Hurtig Publishers, 1982); Gerald Friesen, *The
    Canadian Prairies: A History* (Toronto: University of Toronto
    Press, 1984), chapters one through six; Glyndwr Williams,
    "The Hudson's Bay Company and the Fur Trade: 1670-1870,"
    The Beaver 314 (Autumn 1983): 4-86, see also Glyndwr
    Williams, "Highlights in the History of the First Two
    Hundred Years of the Hudson's Bay Company," *The Beaver*
    301 (Autumn 1970): 4-59; Peter C. Newman, *The Company
    of Adventurers* (Markham, Ontario: Viking, 1985).

3   Edwin E. Rich, "Trade Habits and Economic Motivation
    Among the Indians of North America," *Canadian Journal of
    Economics and Political Science* 26 (1960): 35-63; Abraham
    Rotstein, "Trade and Politics: An Institutional Approach,"
    Western Canadian Journal of Anthropology 3 (1972): 1-28. See
    Hartwell Bowsfield, "Studies in Fur," *Archivaria* 12 (Summer
    1981): 121-26, for a discussion of Rotstein's work. See also,
    for example, Bruce M. White, " 'Give us a Little Milk': The
    Social and Cultural Significance of Gift Giving in the Lake
    Superior Fur Trade," in Thomas C. Buckley, ed., *Rendezvous:
    Selected Papers of the Fourth North American Fur Trade
    Conference, 1981* (St. Paul: North American Fur Trade
    Conference, 1983), 185-98.

4   Calvin Martin, *Keepers of the Game: Indian-Animal Relationships
    and the Fur Trade* (Berkeley: University of California Press,

1978), see also his "Subarctic Indians and Wildlife," in Carol
M. Judd and Arthur J. Ray, eds., *Old Trails and New Directions:
Papers of the Third North American Fur Trade Conference*
(Toronto: University of Toronto Press, 1980), 73-81; Shepard
Krech III, ed., *Indians, Animals and the Fur Trade: A Critique
of Keepers of the Game* (Athens, Georgia: University of Georgia
Press, 1981); Adrian Tanner, *Bringing Home Animals: Religious
Ideology and Mode of Production of the Mistassini Cree Hunters*
(New York: St. Martin's Press, 1979).

5   Arthur J. Ray, "Indians as Consumers in the Eighteenth
    Century," in Judd and Ray, eds., *Old Trails and New Directions*,
    255-71; Arthur J. Ray, "Competition and Conservation in the
    Early Subarctic Fur Trade," *Ethnohistory* 25 (1978): 347-57;
    Arthur J. Ray, *Indians in the Fur Trade: Their Role as Hunters,
    Trappers and Middlemen in the Lands Southwest of Hudson Bay,
    1660-1870* (Toronto: University of Toronto Press, 1974); Arthur
    J. Ray, "The Early Hudson's Bay Company Account Books
    as Sources for Historical Research: An Analysis and
    Assessment," *Archivaria* 1 (Winter 1975-76): 3-38; Arthur J.
    Ray and Donald Freeman, *'Give Us Good Measure': An
    Economic Analysis of Relations Between the Indians and the
    Hudson's Bay Company before 1763* (Toronto: University of
    Toronto Press, 1978).

6   Philip D. Curtain, *Cross-Cultural Trade in World History*
    (Cambridge: Cambridge University Press, 1984). See chapter
    ten.

7   Daniel Francis and Toby Morantz, *Partners in Furs: A History
    of the Fur Trade in Eastern James Bay 1600-1870* (Kingston:
    McGill-Queen's University Press, 1983), and Toby Morantz,
    "Economic and Social Accommodations of the James Bay
    Inlanders to the Fur Trade," in Shepard Krech III, ed., *The
    Subarctic Fur Trade: Native Social and Economic Adaptations*
    (Vancouver: University of British Columbia Press, 1984),
    55-80; Charles A. Bishop, *The Northern Ojibway and the Fur
    Trade: An Historical and Ecological Study* (Toronto: Holt,
    Rinehart and Winston of Canada, Ltd., 1974), and "The First
    Century: Adaptive Changes among the Western James Bay
    Cree between the Early Seventeenth and Early Eighteenth
    Centuries," in Krech, ed., *The Subarctic Fur Trade*, 21-54; Robin

Fisher, *Contact and Conflict: Indian-European Relations in British Columbia, 1774-1890* (Vancouver: University of British Columbia Press, 1977). See also Arthur J. Ray, *Indians in the Fur Trade.*

8   Calvin Martin, "Ethnohistory: A Better Way to Write Indian History," *Western Historical Quarterly* 9 (January 1978): 41-56. See also Arthur J. Ray, "Fur Trade History as an Aspect of Native History," in Ian A.L. Getty and Donald B. Smith, eds., *One Century Later: Western Canadian Reserve Indians Since Treaty 7* (Vancouver: University of British Columbia Press, 1978), 7-19; Jacqueline Peterson and John Afinson, "The Indian and the Fur Trade: A Review of Recent Literature," *Manitoba History* 10 (Autumn 1985): 10-18; and Donald F. Bibeau, "Fur Trade Literature from a Tribal Point of View: A Critique," in Buckley, ed., *Rendezvous,* 83-92. Useful overviews have also been provided by J.W. St. G. Walker, "The Indian in Canadian Historical Writing," Canadian Historical Association, *Historical Papers* (1971): 21-47, and "The Indian in Canadian Historical Writing, 1972-1982," in I.A.L. Getty and A.S. Lussier, eds., *As Long as the Sun Shines and Water Flows: A Reader in Canadian Native Studies* (Vancouver: University of British Columbia Press, 1983), 340-57; and Bruce G. Trigger, "The Historian's Indian: Native Americans in Canadian Historical Writing from Charlevoix to the Present," *Canadian Historical Review* 67 (September 1986): 315-42.

9   James W. Van Stone, *Athapaskan Adaptations: Hunters and Fishermen of the Subarctic Forests* (Chicago: Aldine, 1974); Krech, ed., *The Subarctic Fur Trade;* Shepard Krech III, "The Trade of the Slavey and Dogrib at Fort Simpson in the Early Nineteenth Century," in Krech, ed., *Subarctic Fur Trade,* 99-146; Arthur J. Ray, "Periodic Shortages, Native Welfare, and the Hudson's Bay Company 1670-1930," in Krech, ed., *Subarctic Fur Trade,* 1-20.

10 J.C. Yerbury, *The Subarctic Indians and the Fur Trade, 1680-1860* (Vancouver: University of British Columbia Press, 1986); June Helm, E. Rogers and J.G.E. Smith, "Intercultural Relations and Cultural Change in the Shield and Mackenzie Borderlands," in W.E. Sturtevant, gen. ed., *Handbook of North*

American Indians, Volume 6: Subarctic (Washington, D.C.: Smithsonian Institution, 1981), 146-57. See also, for example, June Helm et al., "The Contact History of the Subarctic Athapaskans: An Overview," in Annette M. Clark, ed., *Proceedings: Northern Athapaskan Conference 1971*, vol. 1 (Ottawa: National Museums of Canada, 1975), 302-48; Shepard Krech III, *Native Canadian Anthropology and History: A Selected Bibliography* (Winnipeg: Rupert's Land Research Centre, 1986).

11 Jennifer H. Brown, *Strangers in Blood: Fur Trade Company Families in Indian Country* (Vancouver: University of British Columbia Press, 1980).

12 Sylvia Van Kirk, *"Many Tender Ties": Women in Fur Trade Society in Western Canada, 1670-1870* (Winnipeg: Watson and Dwyer Ltd., 1980), and Sylvia Van Kirk, "Thanadelthur," *The Beaver* 304.4 (1974): 40-45; Richard J. Perry, "The Fur Trade and the Status of Women in the Western Subarctic," *Ethnohistory* 26 (1979); Jennifer H. Brown, "Children of the Early Fur Trades," in Joy Parr, ed., *Childhood and Family in Canadian History* (Toronto: McClelland and Stewart Ltd., 1982), 44-68.

13 Jacqueline Peterson and Jennifer H. Brown, *The New Peoples: Being and Becoming Métis in North America* (Winnipeg: University of Manitoba Press, 1985). See also Arthur J. Ray, "Reflections on Fur Trade Social History and Métis History in Canada," *American Indian Culture and Research Journal* 6, no. 2 (1982): 91-107. It should be mentioned here that Marcel Giraud's seminal study of the Métis is now available in an English translation: Marcel Giraud, George Woodcock, trans., *The Métis in the Canadian West* (Edmonton: University of Alberta Press, 1986).

14 John E. Foster, "The Métis: The People and the Term," *Prairie Forum* 3, no. 1 (1978): 79-90; Jennifer H. Brown, "Women as Centre and Symbol in the Emergence of Métis Communities," *Canadian Journal of Native Studies* 3, no. 1 (1983): 39-46. See also Jacqueline Peterson, "The People in Between: Indian-White Marriage and the Genesis of a Métis Society and Culture in the Great Lakes Region, 1680-1830" (Ph.D. dissertation, University of Illinois at Chicago, 1981),

and Peterson, "Ethnogenesis: The Settlement and Growth of a 'New People' in the Great Lakes Region, 1702-1815," *American Indian Culture and Research Journal* 6, no. 2 (1982): 23-64; Olive P. Dickason, "From 'One Nation' in the Northeast to 'New Nation' in the Northwest: A Look at the Emergence of the Métis," *American Indian Culture and Research Journal* 6, no. 2 (1982), 1-21; Carol Judd, "Mixed Bloods of Moose Factory, 1730-1981: A Socio-economic Study," *American Indian Culture and Research Journal* 6, no. 2 (1982): 65-88; Sylvia Van Kirk, " 'What if Mama is an Indian?': The Cultural Ambivalence of the Alexander Ross Family," in Peterson and Brown, eds., *The New Peoples*, 206-17.

15 Much of the literature exists in article form. Only a few are given here: Bruce Cox, "Indian Middlemen and the Early Fur Trade: Reconsidering the Position of the Hudson's Bay Company's 'Trading Indians,'" in Buckley, ed., *Rendezvous*, 93-100; Greg Thomas and Ian Clarke, "The Garrison Mentality and the Canadian West," *Prairie Forum* 4, no. 1 (1979): 83-104; John F. Taylor, "Socio-Cultural Effects of Epidemics on the Northern Plains: 1734-1850," *Western Canadian Journal of Anthropology* 7, no. 4 (1977): 55-81; Arthur J. Ray, "Competition and Conservation in the Early Subarctic Fur Trade," *Ethnohistory* 25, no. 4 (1978): 347-57; Judd and Ray, eds., *Old Trails*, and Buckley, ed., *Rendezvous*.

16 D.W. Moodie, "Agriculture and the Fur Trade," in Judd and Ray, eds., *Old Trails*, 272-90; D.W. Moodie and Barry Kaye, "Indian Agriculture in the Fur Trade Northwest," *Prairie Forum* 11, no. 2 (1986): 171-83; Philip Goldring, "Employment Relations in the Fur Trade, 1821-1892," paper presented at the annual meeting, Canadian Historical Association, June 1981; Philip Goldring, "Governor Simpson's Officers: Elite Recruitment in a British Overseas Enterprise, 1834-1870," *Prairie Forum* 10, no. 2 (1985): 251-81; A.A. Den Otter, "Transportation and Transformation: The Hudson's Bay Company, 1857-1885," *Great Plains Quarterly* (Summer 1983): 171-85; Eric W. Morse, *Fur Trade Canoe Routes/Then and Now*, 2nd ed. (Ottawa: Queen's Printer, 1979).

17 John S. Galbraith, *The Little Emperor: Governor Simpson of the Hudson's Bay Company* (Toronto: Macmillan, 1976); Marjorie Wilkins Campbell, *Northwest to the Sea: A Biography of William*

McGillivray (Toronto: Clarke, Irwin, 1975); Adrian Tanner, "The End of Fur Trade History," *Queen's Quarterly* 90, no. 1 (Spring 1983): 176-91. H.A. Innis's monumental study, *The Fur Trade in Canada: An Introduction to Canadian Economic History* (Toronto: University of Toronto Press, 1936), remains the only theoretical economic synthesis to treat the entire fur trade period.

18 C.A. Bishop and Arthur J. Ray, "Ethnohistorical Research in the Central Subarctic: Some Conceptual and Methodological Problems," *Western Canadian Journal of Anthropology* 6, no. 1 (1976): 116-44; R.R. Janes, "The Athapascan and the Fur Trade: Observations from Archeology and Ethnohistory," *Western Canadian Journal of Anthropology* 5, nos.3-4 (1975): 159-86; W.A. Sloan, "The Native Response to the Extension of the European Traders into the Athabasca and Mackenzie Basin, 1770-1814," *Canadian Historical Review* 60, no. 3 (1979): 281-99; James G.E. Smith, "Chipewyan, Cree and Inuit Relations West of Hudson Bay, 1714-1955," *Ethnohistory* 28, no. 2 (1981): 133-57; Robert A. Wuetherick, *A History of Fort Chipewyan and the Peace-Athabasca Delta Region* (Edmonton: n.p., 1972); Eric Krause, "The Fisheries of the Hudson's Bay Company at Fort Chipewyan, 1791-1871," Manuscript Report Series no. 208 (Ottawa: Parks Canada, 1976); Patricia McCormack, "How the (North) West was Won: Development and Underdevelopment in the Fort Chipewyan Region" (Ph.D. dissertation, University of Alberta, 1984).

19 Karlis Karklins, "Nottingham House: The Hudson's Bay Company in Athabasca 1802-1806," History and Archeology Series no. 69 (Ottawa: Parks Canada, 1983); Robert S. Allen, "Peter Fidler and Nottingham House, Lake Athabasca 1802-1806," History and Archeology Series no. 69 (Ottawa: Parks Canada, 1983); Donald N. Steer, "The History and Archeology of a North West Company Trading Post and a Hudson's Bay Company Transport Depot, Lac La Loche, Saskatchewan," Manuscript Report no. 280 (Ottawa: Parks Canada, 1977); Robert S. Kidd, "Fort George and the Early Fur Trade in Alberta," Provincial Museum and Archives of Alberta Publication no. 2 (Edmonton: Provincial Museum and Archives of Alberta, 1970); Norman F. Barka and Anne

Barka, "Archeology and the Fur Trade: The Excavation of Sturgeon Fort, Saskatchewan," History and Archeology Series no. 7 (Ottawa: Parks Canada, 1976). See also, for example, Gerhard Ens and Barry Potyondi, "A History of the Upper Athabasca Valley in the Nineteenth Century" (Calgary: Great Plains Research Consultants, 1986); and William C. Noble, "The Excavation and Historical Identification of Rocky Mountain House," Occasional Papers in Archeology and History no. 6 (Ottawa: Canadian Historic Sites, 1973).

20 Kenneth E. Kidd and Martha A. Kidd, "A Classification System for Glass Beads for the Use of Field Archaeologists," Occasional Papers in Archeology and History no. 1 (Ottawa: Canadian Historic Sites, 1970); N. Jaye Frederickson, "The Covenant Chain: Indian Ceremonial and Trade Silver," catalogue of the travelling exhibition of the National Museum of Man by Sandra Gibb (Ottawa: The National Museum of Man, 1980); Lester A. Ross, "A Guide to the Description of Axes," unpublished manuscript (Ottawa: Parks Canada, 1977); Robert C. Wheeler et al., *Voices from the Rapids: An Underwater search for Fur Trade Artifacts, 1960-73* (St. Paul: Minnesota Historical Society, 1975).

Proper Name Index

G

H

I

J

K

L

M

Geographical Index

B

Bark River, 112
Beaverlodge, 1
Berens, 117
Big Island. *See* Bustard Island
Big Point Channel, 31
Birch Mountain, 62
Black River, 15
Bolsover House, 15
Burnside River, 1
Burntwood River, 12, 15
Bustard Island, 31, 49

C

Calumet River, 61
Carribeau Lake, 85
Chesterfield House, 15
Chesterfield Inlet, 11
Christina River, 11
Churchill Fort, 6, 7, 11, 14, 15, 21, 83, 84, 126
Churchill River, 4-6, 12, 15, 29, 83
Claire Lake. *See* Lake Claire
Clear Lake. *See* Lake Claire
Clearwater River, 6, 11, 28, 29
Coal Island. *See* Potato Island
Cochrane River, 15
Cracroft River, 1
Cumberland House, 6, 11, 14, 15, 29, 45, 50, 60, 64, 73, 126

D

Dog Head, 4, 32, 34
Dunvegan, 51, 60, 136

E

Elk River, 112
Embarras River, 28, 29, 32, 33, 57
English Island, 4, 15, 34, 35, 51
English River, 130, 145
Essex House, 15

F

Fairford House, 15
Fidler Point, 33
Fond du Lac, 60, 112, 142
Fort Chipewyan, 1, 4, 11-13, 25, 33-38, 40, 41, 43-47, 51, 52, 54, 58, 60-62, 64, 67, 76-78, 82-84, 86, 94, 95, 101, 103, 104, 112, 113, 115-17, 125, 130, 132, 133, 136, 137, 140, 141, 143-44, 146, 185, 186

Fort de l'Isle, 20
Fort de Pinnette, 51
Fort Detroit, 114
Fort Michillimakkinak, 114
Fort Simpson, 188
Fort Smith, 93
Fort St. John's, 136, 137
Fort Vermilion, 51, 60, 132, 136
Fort Wedderburn, 4, 22, 35, 36, 40, 92, 114, 130, 132, 133
Fort William, 72, 132
Frog Portage, 6

G

Garson Lake, 11
Garson River, 11
Goose Island, 4, 31, 47
Grand Portage, 45, 114
Great Bear Lake, 1
Great Slave Lake, 10, 11, 30, 31, 33, 60, 62, 76, 84, 95, 112, 134, 136, 137
Green Lake, 15
Greenwich House, 15

H

Hay River, 112
Hudson Bay, 4, 6, 7, 13, 14, 20, 29, 73, 83, 84, 131

I

Ile-à-la-Crosse, 5, 11, 15, 29, 30, 34, 55, 85
Ile-à-la Crosse, 5, 29

L

Lac la Biche, 15
Lac la Biche River, 15
Lac la Pluie, 104, 115, 132
Lac la Ronge, 10
Lake Athabasca, 1, 6, 11, 15, 18, 21, 25, 30-32, 46, 61, 62, 64, 67, 84
Lake Claire, 25, 32, 55, 57, 60, 112, 142
Lake Winnipeg, 114, 145
Lesser Slave Lake River, 15
Little Island, 4, 18, 35
Little Poplar Island, 31
London, 12, 20, 69, 143

M

Mackenzie River, 1, 12, 33, 62, 76, 113, 123, 134, 136, 137, 146, 192
Maligne River, 73

S

Saleesh House, 43
Salt Plains, 55
Salt River, 50
Saskatchewan River, 4-6, 11, 14, 34, 45
Sault Ste. Marie, 13
Slave River, 1, 11, 50, 55, 75, 93, 104
South Saskatchewan River, 15
Sturgeon Fort, 6

W

Wager Bay, 11
Wollaston Lake, 15

Y

York Factory, 7, 14, 15, 42, 62, 123, 137